It IS what you say!

Increase your profits with the power of your communication.

The money is in your message.

James McGinty

Bespeak
1/1, 119 Neilston Road
Paisley PA2 6ER
Renfrewshire
Scotland

www.itiswhatyousay.com

ISBN No 978-1532955723

Foreword

Do you want your business to flourish and see its profits increase? Of course you do!

In this book *"It **IS** What You Say",* James McGinty will take you on a journey through all levels of business communication and beyond to ensure that your vision thrives and your profits grow.

As a trainer and professional speaker, James works with people like you in every level of business, from the tiny start up to corporate giants, including most of the FTSE 100 and many of the Fortune 500 companies.

James is a communication skills expert and by reading this book you will benefit hugely from the knowledge he will share with you. James does not simply talk about communication skills; he provides practical examples using real life stories that give expert guidance on business communication strategy and implementation.

This book is a necessary read for you to make sure that every employee within your business, every customer that buys from you, and every supplier that you work with understands the vision that drives your company and helps to make it a reality.

Raymond Aaron

New York Times Bestselling Author

Acknowledgments

I see many books with pages of acknowledgements, as many people are needed to help bring a book to life.

I have one simple acknowledgment to make. It is to my wife Margaret.

Margaret lives with Alzheimer's dementia and does not always have a clear picture of what is going on in the world around her but always has a happy smile.

Throughout the process of writing this book, she may not have understood what I was doing, but she recognised my passion. She gave up days out, put up with me working while on holiday, and let me turn her world upside down without a single complaint.

She read every page as it was produced and spotted over 100 mistakes, saving hours of editing. When I worked long into the night, she sat up, bringing me coffee and cookies, and generally made the whole process much easier.

Alzheimer's dementia is a terrible disease, but Margaret has proved, with her support and assistance, that it is possible to live well and contribute even in the most difficult of circumstances.

Margaret, I love and thank you.

Contents

	Foreword	iii
	Acknowledgement	iv
Chapter 1	Your Message Matters	Page 1
Chapter 2	The Language of Communication	Page 16
Chapter 3	Making Sense	Page 30
Chapter 4	Connect With Stories	Page 44
Chapter 5	Life With PowerPoint	Page 61
Chapter 6	Mission or Vision	Page 76
Chapter 7	Wizards and Warriors	Page 89
Chapter 8	Breaking the Chain	Page 104
Chapter 9	Empowering Your People	Page 116
Chapter 10	What Don't You Know	Page 133
	About the Author	Page 147

Chapter 1 Your Message Matters

The message from the boardroom

All business communications should start from the top. It is the CEO's job to make sure that they are creating the company messages. I appreciate that smaller businesses may not have a boardroom or even a board as such, but even if you are a sole trader, when creating a message, you have to think like a corporate CEO.

Every business is its message, and the message is the business. It does not matter what your company does or what your products or services are. Physical items, virtual items or services can only produce profits if your customers want to buy them and you have a contented workforce prepared to make or source them.

Any message that comes from the boardroom has to be a deliberate, conscious message. It needs to be precise and easy for everyone to understand so there is no doubt about what the message is or what its purpose is.

Imagine that as the CEO, you walk through the office one morning and notice it's a real mess with overflowing bins, crumbs on the floor and desks covered in bundles of paper, dirty cups and snack wrappers, and the whole place looks totally unprofessional.

You could tell the people directly to get it tidied up. That would probably work for about ten minutes, an hour or maybe even a day or two, depending on how strongly you make your case.

Because the message was an off the cuff, instant reaction to a situation, chances are the message hasn't been fully thought through or expressed in the clearest terms.

In cases like this, especially when it can appear to some as trivial, the message gets gradually diluted and disappears.

If an untidy office is an issue that needs to be resolved, and generally it is, then the message needs to be crafted and explained. This has to happen at the top so that everyone from the CEO down knows what is expected and why.

If there is a rest area, then you might have a policy that says no eating or drinking at desks. Smaller companies don't generally provide a rest area, so you may have a policy that states all cups must be washed and put away at the end of the day. You also need to state why.

If you are goin-g to give even a few minutes of expensive boardroom time to something as mundane as office cleanliness and tidiness, you need to think out your message beforehand. Make sure you can say what the new policy should be and why it should be that way. Think about the possible objections and have rebuttals ready for them.

Listen carefully to what others in the boardroom have to say and, if necessary, adjust the message. Hopefully as you have already given a lot of thought to the message, any changes that need to be made will be minor, and your message can be put out to the organisation.

I have used a trivial example here for clarity because it is a situation that anyone can envisage.

Every business will have different and bigger challenges, but if they are treated in the same consistent way and all messages are delivered clearly and with purpose, then you will have a workforce who are consistently behaving in a way that is congruent with the company's goals and objectives.

Communication in the organisation

Now that you have created your message. How do you communicate it throughout your organisation?

This is a multi-stage process, and each stage needs to be handled differently but done in parallel. It's easy to write something like:

"Clear desk policy; for reasons of efficiency and safety, it has been decided to implement a clear desk and general tidiness policy. No cups, plates, food, wrappers, etc. are to be left on or in desks after close of business. All paperwork and client folders should be returned to cabinets and filed correctly at the end of each day."

However, if you, the CEO, email this to everyone, it's likely to look like micromanagement, unless you are in a small company, in which case it may well be OK.

If you have taken the time and trouble to discuss something like this, then take the time and trouble to document it. Every organisation, no matter how large or small, should have an employee handbook.

I have always liked a tidy desk (but with a coffee cup) and at one company, where my department only had two people, my new colleague looked at my desk and asked if the company had a clear desk policy. I had to say that I didn't know, as no one had told me and there was no company handbook.

It became a secondary role for me to create one and once done, new updates only took a few minutes. With each update, I sent an email out to people detailing the change and providing a link to the updated handbook on the company network.

Make sure you delegate someone to create and maintain your company handbook and that each time a policy is updated or a new policy is decided upon, every member of staff is made aware of it.

In parallel with this, any message that has been deemed worthy of boardroom time, needs to be conveyed in a more personal, face to face manner.

One of the biggest complaints in large companies is that the workforce is too far removed from the management. In smaller companies, receiving a memo or email from a boss that is sitting in the next office, will often cause resentment because, "it would only take a minute to pop their head round the door and tell us."

Regular staff or departmental meetings are the best way to keep staff happy and make them feel they are part of the decision making process. Meetings need to be regular and adhered to.

I have worked for several companies that professed to have a staff meeting every month, but in reality they happened about once every 3 – 4 months, or when a big policy decision was being handed down from on high.

This made me feel isolated from team leaders or management in these scenarios. I noticed that staff ganged together and ran things their own way. This kept them happy but off message and not working towards the organisation's best interests.

Never let your regular meetings slip. They are the best method for communicating within any business and go a long way in making sure your message is heard, understood, and acted upon.

It may be worth arranging these meetings so that there is a social component to them.

Perhaps a small buffet lunch can be provided immediately after a monthly meeting. The manager could have a budget to buy the first round of drinks in the bar after an evening meeting; at the very least, free coffee and biscuits should be provided.

Be careful not to let the social side interfere with the business of the meeting. Also be careful that any social choice you make does not alienate any employee or group of employees.

I recall an employee who was seen as anti-social because she always dashed out of the office at 5:00 pm and never went for after work drinks. The reason was simple. If she missed her train, then she also missed a branch line connection, and a 30-minute commute turned into a 3-hour journey home. A social reward of after meetings drinks would not work for her.

These meetings need to have minutes taken and distributed to all who attended and to the appropriate management chain. These minutes serve as a record that the meeting happened, that the content of the meeting discussed the appropriate matters and that all attendees agreed about what was decided, even if they weren't 100% happy with all of the decisions.

Your message to customers

Your business messages are exceptionally important within your organisation. The messages that come down from the boardroom are ultimately what should shape company culture. However, if, as described previously, you don't document your messages and policies and don't hold regular departmental meetings to keep your staff informed and involved, a counter culture will quickly evolve.

This counter culture will become the de facto culture, where employees will run their day to day tasks in a way that suits them rather than the way the company should be run.

Worse still, your employees are often the people who talk to your customers on a day to day basis. It is the interactions with these employees that will shape your customers' opinion of your organisation. It will also influence their decisions as to whether they will buy goods or services from you in the future.

For example, if your message regarding customer interaction is that you will always answer the telephone on or before the third ring (a surprisingly common policy, but why not on the first ring?), I can guarantee that this is what your sales force will tell customers.

"We always answer the phone on or before the third ring, and it is almost always before it." Why would they say anything else? It's company policy, and they want to make the sale.

If you have good communication inside your organisation and the "third ring" policy is part of the company culture, it will almost always be answered before the third ring.

Poor communication ensures ending up with a counter culture; it is almost certain that the earliest a phone will be answered is on the fourth ring because everyone will be waiting for someone else to answer it.

There can be a fast downward spiral. I once worked for an organisation where there was this sort of counter culture, and somehow I became part of it. The phone would ring and suddenly people were busy looking at their computer screens or delving into a filing cabinet. Everyone waited to see if someone else would answer the phone. We were aware of the third ring policy, and when the third ring happened, I would normally give in and answer it on the fourth ring.

I ended up answering most of the calls and started to become resentful that I was doing more work than anyone else in the office. My attitude changed, and if I was genuinely busy, I stopped breaking from my current task to get the phone on the fourth ring. Of course, everyone was surprised when I did not answer on that fourth ring and that meant it was five, six or seven rings before the phone was answered.

Customer complaints started to trickle in, and after a few weeks, this became a flood. The complaints went to the account managers who would ask us to *"answer the phone as quickly as possible."* We of course genuinely felt that this was what we were doing. It was not until we started losing customers that someone on high intervened. The issue was eventually resolved but in a way that left employees feeling resentful and problems began to surface elsewhere.

It became a poor environment to work in and I, and a few others, moved on to pastures new. The company still exists today and, having talked to an ex-employee who is still close to someone that works there, they have a huge staff turnover and are constantly losing customers.

This is a typical example of where a clear message from the top of the organisation falls flat. "The phone will be answered on or before the third ring" is not communicated clearly enough to the people who are responsible for implementing it. Consequently, the message is diluted and becomes, "Answer the phone as quickly as possible."

At one relatively small company, our CEO wanted everyone's time to be more accountable and decided that we would have to record everything we did in 15-minute blocks.

He expressed this to our training director as follows. *"I was at a meeting today, and others in the industry have their staff recording their time in 15 minute blocks. I want that implemented here."*

The director in turn passed this on to the manager as follows. *"George has been at a meeting, and now he is planning to have us recording time in 15 minute blocks"*

The manager told the team leader, *"Sally says we might have to record everything that we do in the future, so can you buy some record sheets with 15 minute intervals on it?"*

The team leader bought the record sheets but did not even tell the trainers about them, as he was waiting for instructions on full implementation.

Consequently, what seemed like a clear message at the top had no impact at the bottom. It was weeks before the CEO decided to follow up, and he was quite shocked to find that nothing had been done. I left that organisation eighteen months later, and time was still not being recorded.

With few exceptions, employees do not set out to damage the company, but if your message is not clear and precise to your employees, they will send their version of your message out to your customers. Unless you are lucky, considerable damage will be done to the company as a result.

For many years, I worked in the computer applications training industry. I saw many companies close because they lost customers due to staff not adhering to policies that their sales teams had told the customers to expect.

Your message to suppliers

Suppliers are as important as customers and fall into three categories.

1. Those who provide goods and services to you. This type of supplier may provide your office stationary or parts for machines you manufacture. They may also supply services like office cleaning, air conditioning servicing, etc.

2. Those who provide infrastructure services like telephony, internet or delivery services. These services can portray an image of you to your customers that enhance or detract from your reputation.

3. Contractors who act on your behalf and interface directly with your clients, who are likely to view them as if they were directly employed by you.

All three of these groups need to be on board with your company message, especially when it comes to the quality that you have promised your customers.

Being operations manager for a major training company in London, I found it difficult to find a high quality cleaning service. Due to the competitive nature of the cleaning business, everyone was used to competing on price.

Whenever I interviewed prospective companies, they promised me whatever I asked for but never delivered. They found it impossible to do a good job at the prices they were quoting because they were paying staff a minimum (sometimes less) wage and their staff had no motivation.

I eventually found a company who understood the company message about needing to have exceptionally clean premises, as we were client focused.

I had to pay a bit more, but by working closely with the company and interacting with their cleaning staff, I got the quality that I had promised to our customers.

The second group can be quite tricky as choices are limited, and it is impossible to exercise full control over infrastructure services. The best advice is to do some research and find companies with high ratings. A good quality reseller will provide you with an account manager, and when there are problems, they will work with the provider to resolve your issue quickly.
If your account manager knows a bit about your business, and how important the services are to you and your customers, they will know how likely you are to seek another supplier if they cannot provide you with good service levels.

There is a tendency to think that all suppliers are the same and to make a choice on price alone. I used a major courier company to deliver training materials to our customers in advance of courses held at their premises.

The drivers were always polite, dressed in tidy uniforms, and drove nice clean vans. We were happy with their service until we received a complaint from a customer. It turned out that our nationally respected courier company was redistributing our packages via a network of low paid contractors.

One of these had turned up at a FTSE 100 company in the city, dressed in dirty shorts and a vest, smelling of stale food, cigarette smoke and foul body odour. It took a lot of hard work to retain that customer.

The contractors that work directly for you and provide services directly to clients will almost certainly be seen as employees; therefore, you need to treat them as such.

You need to have an induction process that lets contractors know the level and quality of service that you provide to your clients and ensure that they understand that you are the outstanding company in your field and that this has to be reflected in their work.

If left to their own devices, most contractors will provide a good service, but it will be to their standards and not yours. If it is not possible to physically meet with a contractor, a telephone call or skype session with them should be followed up by a copy of the contractor handbook (you have got one of those haven't you?) that explains in writing everything that is expected of them and backs up the conversation you had.
If you source your contractors through an agency, make sure that someone in your organisation is holding regular face-to-face meetings with the management of the agency. This personal touch will build a stronger relationship and ensure that you get the best service possible.

In all of these cases, you might have to pay a little more - sometimes in money, but often in time and effort - to get the quality you need, but quality service always leads to higher profits, so it is worth doing.

Changing the message

I said at the start of this chapter that your message is the business and the business is the message.

What you say and what you do need to be congruent at all times. When your business focus changes, often the actions will start to differ from the spoken or written message.

Every business should be growing, changing and maturing so the messages from the top should be changing as well. Employees are astute and will often sense the changes before they hear about them, and the rumour mill will start to grind.

I once worked for an accounting software company. They had always specialised in one highly acclaimed software package. Most of my work was in training end users, but I spend about 10% of my time programming bespoke interfaces for customers.

It was a relatively small company, and I soon got wind that the sales force was promoting a new package. I, and others in the training and development team, were concerned for our jobs and debated the implications in the break room and in the bar after work. One employee was insecure and left as soon as soon as he could find a new post.

The rest of us worked on in an unpleasant atmosphere until I decided to approach the CEO and ask some questions. It turns out that the company had been given an opportunity to sell a different product, but in a different market segment. This was going to lead to more job security, some upskilling and a stronger company.

All the pain and anxiety that we had gone through was unnecessary, and another team member left due to the lack of information coming from the top. It would have taken no more than five minutes for our CEO to call a quick meeting and explain what was happening. There may well have been a little insecurity, but it would have been far less, and I doubt that we would have lost two members of staff.

As the internet continues to impact businesses, sometimes in unexpected ways, communicating change is vitally important for large organisations. I have lost count of the number of times I heard employees say, *"The first I knew about it was when a friend in another office tweeted it"* or something similar.

If you are a bricks and mortar retailer and are about to change your focus to online sales, let your staff know as soon as possible and certainly well before the media gets a hold of your year-end figures and start drawing wrong conclusions.

If you have created a business plan that entails shutting some stores, let the people in those stores know in a controlled fashion as soon as you can. Remember as soon as two people know something, it cannot be kept secret, and the rumour mill will always churn out the wrong story.

You may well lose some employees in the process and face staffing challenges in those branches earmarked for closure, but if the rumour gets out before the facts, you will lose even more employees and face staffing challenges even in the branches you intend to keep open.

When you do tell your employees of impending closures and job losses, make sure you include a message that they should be giving to customers. If you are a retailer closing stores and changing your focus to online sales, make sure your staff is collecting email addresses and giving out money off vouchers for the first online purchase.

Let the customers know that they will still get the quality and service they are used to but in a different fashion.

Let your supply chain know that you will still be using them and expect them to maintain their quality and pricing. If you are going to require faster deliveries or are changing to a drop-shipping model, let your suppliers know. If you think you will need to change suppliers, let your existing suppliers know as soon as possible. They may be willing to change their practices and pricing in order to keep your business.

Whatever changes you are implementing, you need to think through the ramifications for everyone your company is involved with. Create the message or messages that will result in the best outcome for all concerned, then deliver them with confidence and clarity at the earliest opportunity.

Chapter 1 Summary

Communication always has to be a two-way street. Every time you send out a message, it is likely that at least one person will fail to understand the message or misinterpret it. You do not have to be too concerned if only one or two people do not get it. If the majority of the message recipients understand, then it is probably a good message.

Often, a message designed to inform about large changes will not be well received. Hopefully you will have anticipated this and prepared rebuttals for possible questions; this will help people understand that the message, and their response to it, has been thought through.
If you get multiple feedback on a consequence that you have not thought about, then it is essential that this is dealt with quickly and positively. Most often, it will be something minor, and your response will be simple and not in any way alter the intent or outcome of your message. There will be times, hopefully few, when a point will be legitimate and require an alteration or addendum to your new policy.

Take the example of the clear desk policy statement from the beginning of this chapter.

"Clear desk policy. For reasons of efficiency and safety, it has been decided to implement a clear desk and general tidiness policy. No cups, plates, food, wrappers, etc. are to be left on or in desks after close of business. All paperwork and client folders should be returned to cabinets and filed correctly at the end of each day."

Regarding the final sentence, in a large organisation or department, people are likely to come back and say, that if they return the client folder before they complete their work on it, then someone could prematurely start on the next stage of a process with incomplete information.

In a case like this, a swift resolution of making an exception for work in progress should be forthcoming. This should verbally detail the changed procedure (In this case, closing the folder in a drawer or "pending" tray) and be updated in the handbook as soon as possible.

This type of feedback is much easier in the small organisation, but it is also easier in the small business to forget about the documentation as everyone has so many other duties to perform. Remember that if you do not document your policies, they may as well not exist. They will probably be carried out by your current employees, but without guidance, future employees are less likely to adhere to them.

In the larger organisation, it can be a long way from the boardroom to the shop floor, so make sure your senior managers are prepared to read your policies, think through the detail, and come back to you with questions before the message is disseminated company wide. Having people who only take what you decide on board and pass it on will ultimately cause damage to your company culture and in turn to your bottom line.

Being prepared to listen and adapt is crucial to harmony within a company. No matter how experienced or clever you are, you cannot expect to get it right every time. The reason you are in charge of a business, large or small, is probably a mixture of experience, intelligence and tenacity. If you do get unexpected feedback from a message and you listen and still believe that the message or policy, as decided by you and your board or partners, is the right one, then stick with it and make sure that everyone knows that your messages is their message and must be adhered to.

Chapter 2 The Language Of Communication

Why choosing your words is so important

Almost anyone can create a message and pass it on. Most of the time, the people that read your message can understand it. The goal when creating a message is to make sure that it is understood by everyone to whom it is directed.

It is unlikely that everyone who is exposed to your message will understand it, but that still has to be your goal.

When people create messages, they generally suffer from one of two problems. Either they make the message quite vague, assuming that everyone will understand the intention of the message, or they make the message too complex, assuming again that everyone will understand the intent of the message.

It can be difficult for the creator of a message to imagine that anyone could misunderstand what the intent of their message is, but civil courts are constantly filled with lawyers making a living from arguing over what the intent of a message was.

The central theme of the Charles Dickens novel *Bleak House* is a court case (Jarndyce vs Jarndyce) in which the intent of two wills appear to be in conflict. This is said to be based on the true story of William Jennens who died in 1798 and because he omitted to sign his will, a challenge went through the courts even though his intent was thought to be clear.

In both the fictional case and the real case, the proceedings were brought to an end, not with a satisfactory conclusion, but with the estates running out of funds due to legal costs.

In the case of William Jennens, the court case went on for almost 120 years and used up the modern day equivalent of £200 million.

It is highly unlikely that any message you create will lead to a situation quite so bad, but you still need to choose your words carefully.

The business world practically runs on email today. Most companies have a disclaimer stating that no contract can be entered into via email unless it is done in a particular fashion, which will be outlined in the disclaimer.

I do not want to dwell on disclaimers and their effectiveness here (although I know of one case where Du Pont UK lost an action in the Scottish courts despite their disclaimer).

It is clear that the need for these disclaimers has come about due to the casual nature of communication via email (and in some cases skype and other forms of instant messaging).

This casualness in electronic communications is gradually becoming the norm, and as more and more people spend their leisure time (and indeed some business time) on social media, it is inevitable that we have to think carefully to ensure that business messages are carefully crafted to be professional and not open to misinterpretation.

If a message is extremely important (and if it is not, should you be working on it?), make sure you read it several times before you distribute it.

I believe in the peer review process, and I believe that important messages should be reviewed before distribution. Sadly, as the pace of business has increased, this process is falling by the wayside.

In a previous job, a colleague was asked to put together a proposal for a client for him to work from home in his own accountancy business.

That colleague was primarily an accounting software trainer and knew little about hardware and software sales, but as it was for a special client, he agreed to do it. I peer reviewed the proposal and noticed a couple of items that he had missed, but as I was also an accounts trainer, I suggested he pass it to our manager to check before sending it.

He did this, but the manager gave it a perfunctory glance and said he trusted us to get it right.

We had everything right apart from the annual maintenance contract for the software. We were not aware of this, but our boss was and assumed we would have been as well.

This resulted in an awkward conversation with the client twelve months down the line, but it could have been much worse.

We had been ultra-careful to get that message right, as we knew we were out of our comfort zone. The manager should have realised we were out of our comfort zone and made sure that the proposal was fully reviewed by him.

Accentuate the positive

The brain is not good at processing negatives, so always construct your messages in a positive manner whenever possible. If I ask you not to think of an elephant, the first thing that comes to your mind is the image of an elephant.

In order for the brain to deal with any instruction, it has to access everything related to that instruction. It does this in the most efficient way possible.

When I asked you not to think of an elephant, the brain strips off all the unnecessary words and focuses on the main points in the sentence.

What is the object, and what should I do about it? The brain comes up with “elephant” and “think”. Having done this, the brain then processes the other words, but in this case, it is too late; you are already thinking about the elephant.

At school when we are told, “Do not run in the corridors,” we get a mental image of ourselves running and are therefore more likely to do it. It would be much better if we were told to “walk in the corridors.” That way we get a mental image of ourselves walking and are more likely to do it.

During my late teens, I got involved in amateur car racing. I was not popular with the rest of the team as, despite being the best driver (at least in theory), I crashed into the wall on the same bend on many occasions. My teammates gave the following advice: “Don’t look at the wall.”

Of course, every time I came to the bend, I thought, “Don’t look at the wall.” The next thing I did was look at the wall because my brain went through the sentence and pulled the object, “wall,” and what should I do, “look.” Once I looked at the wall, there was a good chance I would drive into it.

One day, I was having an after race coffee with a rival. After chatting for a while about my propensity for hitting that wall, he admitted to having the same issue the previous season.

His advice was, “when you get to the bend, look at the exit.” A simple piece of advice, which won me a few races and reduced the repair bills of the team quite considerably.

Too often, instructions in the office are given in the negative. “Don’t forget to finish that proposal by Friday” can easily be interpreted as “Forget to finish that proposal by Friday” because the brain only process “forget, finish, proposal and Friday.”

When you say "Finish that proposal by Friday," you are much more likely to achieve the desired result as the message is couched in positive terms, and there is no scope for ambiguity.

If you want to make sure that proposals are peer reviewed before they are sent to clients, then you need to make sure you state this in positive terms.

"Do not send any proposals out without having them checked by a colleague" will be broken down by the brain as "send, proposal, without, checked, colleague."

If it is company policy and well enough ingrained in your business process, I am sure it will be adhered to. It is still better to couch the message in the positive as the brain, and of course the owner of the brain, is much more comfortable and efficient with positive messages.

"All proposals must be reviewed by a colleague before being sent" is much clearer and more positive and will be more efficiently processed by the brain.

Developing the art of creating positive statements and messages has a side benefit in that it will turn you into a positive thinker. People react much better to people who talk and act in a positive manner because of the efficiency of processing that I have mentioned.

Constantly having to sift out the negatives and work out the exact meaning of a communication is tiring. People will not realise this on a conscious level, but subconsciously they will avoid negative people and be attracted to positive people simply because communication is less effort.

No ifs, ands or buts

When creating messages, it is important to avoid using conditional words like "if," modifiers like "but" or connectors like "and."

Messages need to have as much clarity as possible. Using conjunctions to connect parts of a sentence adds complexity to a message and is one of the chief causes of confusion for those interpreting the message.

Due to the complexity that may be introduced by the use of conjunctions, it is especially important to avoid conjunctions in verbal communication. The recipient of the communication can only ever re-examine what they believe they heard, rather than what was actually said.

In addition, as there will be no lasting record of the conversation; any review of the communication will, at best, be incomplete.

With written word, the recipient of the communication can always reread it if they are unsure of the meaning. It is then easier to go back to the originator of the message and ask for clarification if they do not fully understand the message. You should still keep the complexity down by avoiding conjunctions wherever possible.

"If" is such a little word and it slips into our language so easily. It is incredibly easy to say, "If you miss the deadline, you will be in trouble," "If you don't leave now you will be late for the meeting," "If you reach your target, you will receive a bonus."

In business, "If" is often used to indicate that an outcome is conditional on an action or behaviour. This introduces uncertainty and fear, which is not conducive to an efficient or happy workplace.

Take the above example of receiving a bonus. "If you reach your target, you will receive a bonus." Subconsciously, we all know that it is not our target as it was set by someone else. That aside, the word "if" clearly makes it conditional and imprints upon the recipient of the message that there is doubt about meeting the target.

"When you reach the target, you will receive a bonus." This is a much better statement. It has a built in assumption that the target will be reached, making it more likely to happen. It also does not imply ownership of the target, removing the subconscious feeling that you are trying to achieve someone else's target.

To most people, "and" is a harmless word that helps group similar items together. "Fish and chips," "hammer and chisel," "bricks and mortar." It is extremely useful for making the complex simpler.

No one ever asks for a measure of gin with some tonic. "Gin and tonic" is so much simpler and concise.

The trouble starts when people get into conversational flow, and they start to link ideas together using "and."

"At today's meeting, we are going to discuss new sales targets and what the bonus structure will be and give you some strategies for how you can meet and exceed those targets".

That is a common business message. It has several components that are all related. Reading it as written above, you will find it a little long-winded but probably understandable. When spoken, something odd happens. The brain can only focus on one thing at a time.

When we speak in sentences, the brain recognises the beginning and end of each item. It can file each one for later retrieval and process them at its leisure.

When we use "and" to link the items together, the brain is not clear about the demarcation between the parts. It therefore gets confused and tries to sort it out.

While the brain is sorting out items one and two, active listening decreases, and the recipient will miss the rest of the statement. Avoid the "ands" by breaking the statement down into manageable chunks.

It also helps if you enumerate how many parts there will be as the brain can prepare the appropriate amount of storage spaces.

"At today's meeting, we are going to discuss three items. 1 - New sales targets. 2- The bonus structure. 3 – Strategies to exceed those targets."

Note that I also changed "meet and exceed" to simply exceed, as any target exceeded will have been met anyway.

The final conjunction I will discuss here is "but." This simple grouping of three letters can cause serious damage as it is often used to negate a previous statement, and the recipient will often only remember what they heard after the "but."

"You had a really good month, *but I know you can do better."* "The company remains profitable *but turnover is down."* "The whole department is performing well *but we need to improve customer care."*

The third statement appears reasonable, leaving everyone thinking that customer care needs to be improved and that this is a good thing.

The trouble with that statement is the first part probably is not true. It is a trite statement made to soften a blow, which probably should not be softened.

The first two statements are typical. A positive statement is made to get the recipient(s) of a message off guard and then hit them with a negative. This almost always demotivates the listener and makes them focus on the negative, which is more likely to generate a negative outcome as noted earlier.

To get rid of the "but," simply reverse the statements and perhaps qualify the statement a little.
When you want to encourage an employee to do better, tell them straight out. "I know you can do better; let's see what we can do to improve on the good month you just had."

This will have a much better impact as it ends with praise, leaving the employee happy and more likely to perform better.

If turnover is down but the company remains profitable, there must be a good reason for it. Perhaps qualify the statement with "as expected, turnover is down." This lets everyone know it is not a surprise. Then finish off by saying why the company remains profitable. "We are much more efficient now, so the company remains profitable."

Don't give yourself a nervous breakdown trying to get rid of every single "if", "but" or "and." They have a necessary part to play in everyday language. Be aware of the possible consequences, and use them only where they are appropriate.

Short is sweet

An American general and chairman of the Joint Chiefs of Staff - John W. Vessey, Jr. said,

"More has been screwed up on the battlefield and misunderstood in the Pentagon because of a lack of understanding of the English language than any other single factor."

One of the reasons for misunderstandings is that we often say too much when it isn't necessary.

Despite being the most complex organ in the human body, the brain sometimes behaves in a quite unsophisticated way. It likes to process information in pieces that are as small as possible.

In the previous section, I used an example to illustrate the over use of "and."

"At today's meeting, we are going to discuss new sales targets and what the bonus structure will be and give you some strategies for how you can meet and exceed those targets."

I went on to produce an easier to digest message.

"At today's meeting we are going to discuss three items. 1 - New sales targets. 2- The bonus structure. 3 – Strategies to exceed those targets."

In the process, it also became seven words shorter, which aids understanding. You will generally find that if you think about your message and only write or say the essential parts of what you mean, you will end up with much shorter messages.

People's brains are good at working out detail from the simplest of statements.

Remember the "elephant" example from earlier. When I mention the word elephant, you don't just get a picture of one. You will most likely give it context. You may picture it in a zoo or a safari park. You may picture it wild in the jungle. You may even picture yourself riding on one if this is something you experienced previously.

If you are about to have a sales meeting, and everyone attending has been at previous meetings or have worked in sales for any length of time, they will understand that when you talk about targets and bonuses, there is going to be a discussion around strategies and exceeding them.

It would be unsafe to say "We are having a sales meeting" as a lack of context is still dangerous.

"At today's meeting we are going to discuss targets and bonuses" is probably enough to set the scene for anyone who is attending the meeting. This does go against the principle of precision in message that I wrote about earlier. I would certainly make sure that there was an agenda written out that included each discussion point just to keep people on track and help them follow the progress of the meeting.

Again, short is sweet.

AGENDA

Item 1	This month's targets
Item 2	New bonus structure
Item 3	Strategies

The verbal introduction *"At today's meeting, we are going to discuss targets and bonuses"* coupled with a simple agenda will give everyone a clear idea of what is going on without any confusion or doubt.

This leads to better meetings with more positive outcomes. The efficiency of shorter communications will lead to more efficient meetings, and as the people within your business become used to the style, it will become pervasive, making for a more efficient and profitable business.

Jargon and buzz words

Have you ever been brave enough to play "Buzzword Bingo" (it has a few other names, mostly offensive) in a meeting? The other senior managers and I at a large London company decided to play it for a laugh as our CEO constantly used jargon and meaningless buzzwords.

It is simple. Everyone gets a card like the one below, and each time a word or phrase on the card is mentioned, you cross it out. If you get five in a row (horizontal, vertical or diagonal), you shout BINGO!

synergy	strategic fit	gap analysis	best practice	bottom line
revisit	bandwidth	hardball	out of the loop	benchmark
value-added	proactive	win-win	think outside the box	fast track
result-driven	empower	knowledge base	total quality	touch base
mindset	client focus	ball park	game plan	leverage

I won the first game, as it turned out I was the only person courageous (or stupid) enough to call out. The CEO discovered what we had being doing, and he was a little miffed.

Eventually, he did see both the funny and serious sides of it. Afterwards, he made an effort to use straightforward language at meetings.

To be fair, some of the terms in the card above are OK. I quite like "proactive" and empower." While I fully understand what is meant by "touch base," it is imprecise, and if you ask someone to "touch base on the issue," it is not going to be taken seriously.

The other thing to avoid is the use of industry specific jargon or abbreviations with clients outside of your industry.

Having spent many years in the IT industry, I have been witness to hundreds of conversations where the mention of RAM, ROM, DNS, MX, SPF, Megabytes and Gigabytes have left customers sitting glassy eyed wondering what on earth the person opposite was talking about.

Customers do not care about your jargon or technical specifications. What your customer cares about is being told in the simplest way possible, exactly what the benefit will be to them if they buy your product or service.

Chapter 2 Summary

How people react to your communication should always be observed.

Facial expressions and body language can tell you a lot about how well your message was received. Few people will actively hide their body language or fake expressions; we all have natural first reactions to what we hear.

When speaking, actively observe those to whom you are speaking. If your message is being well received, people will look in your direction, appear interested and tend to be sitting upright. They may not have big happy smiles on their faces, but they will not be scowling either.

Watch for people doodling on notepads and slouching in their chairs; this generally means that they have no real interest in what you have to say. They may well be facing towards you and appear to be listening, but a slouched or overly relaxed posture is often an indicator that someone is daydreaming and therefore not getting the message.

A stiff posture and stony face constantly looking straight at you indicates displeasure and chances are this body language is from someone who disagrees with your message or is confused by it and is trying to make sense of it as you speak.

It is not always possible to adjust your message on the fly. Often, it is a case of observing the reaction to your message and then reviewing your performance afterwards.

If you get a sense that your message is not going over as well as you expected, you should examine it thoroughly using the subheadings from this chapter.

Did you choose the best words and phrases for your message?
Did you present your message in a positive rather than negative fashion?
Did you avoid unnecessary conjunctions to keep the message from being confusing?
Did you keep your sentences short and precise?
Did you avoid Buzzwords and jargon?

If you can honestly answer yes to those five questions and your message is not getting through to the majority of people, then it is likely that your speaking style needs adjusting. It is more likely that it will be one or two people that you are not connecting with.

This is often because different people engage in different ways, and you are not yet specifically targeting each person's listening style. We will look at that in the next chapter.

Chapter 3 Making Sense

Adapt and flourish

"It would be a very dull world if we were all the same," or some derivative of it, is a much over used comment. If you think about it in any depth at all, if we were all the same, we would cease to exist. Evolution is wholly dependent on diversity.

Humankind got to where it is now through the principal of survival of the fittest. That does not necessarily mean that only the strongest survive. It means that the most adaptable (i.e. those who have the best fit for any particular situation) will inevitably be the most successful.

Without this adaptability, we might still be hunter-gatherers, farming would not exist and the wheel would not have been invented. Humankind as we know it could have died out in the same way as the Neanderthals did, due to their inability to adapt.

Humankind has been around in a sort of civilised fashion for about 40,000 years. For most of that time, nothing much changed. It took over 30,000 years for us to come up with the invention of the wheel. From there, developments have come faster and faster. Now, only those at the leading edge and prepared to adapt will be successful.
It is the same with business in the modern world. Adaptability is the key to success. If I were a gambler, I would offer good odds that few readers of this book work for the same company that they did when they left school, college or university. Even fewer will be at the same job they started in.

My first job on leaving school was as an apprentice welder in the Clyde shipyards in Scotland. Fortunately, I could see that there was no future in UK shipbuilding and moved on to pastures new.

There is only one shipyard left on the Clyde and only a handful in the whole of the UK. The amazing thing is that in the thirty years since most of the shipyards closed, the people who lived in those areas have adapted to new jobs and new ways of life.

Many historic companies have disappeared. In the UK, the heart of the industrial revolution, if you ignore pubs, inns and hotels, there are less than fifty UK businesses more than 300 years old.

Thousands of businesses close around the world every year, but people adapt and most industrial or post-industrial countries have unemployment rates in single figures.

In most cases, adaptability is forced on people when external factors affect them. Most people keep moving along the same path until someone or something knocks them off. Only then do they reassess their progress and make changes.

As a business owner or manager, there is a good chance that you got where you are by design rather than happenstance. Many of you have had a life changing experience but you handled it with eyes wide open and controlled your route thereafter.

You need to be in control of your communication skills in the same way. Once you have a destination in mind for your business, it is your communication, with partners, employees, clients, customers and suppliers, that will determine how well and how quickly you reach that destination.

You need to adapt to peoples listening abilities and determine how they will best receive your message and adapt your style to suit. As a communicator, it is your job to ensure that listeners receive and understand your Message.

It is your message, and you need to ensure that you get it, not just into the conscious minds of your listeners, but ingrained in their subconscious so that they will act on your message because they think it is the right thing to do.

I started this chapter by saying, "It would be a very dull world if we were all the same." In fact, we are more the same than we are different.

Healthy humans share around 99.5% of their DNA. Consequently, we tend to treat people as if they are the same as us. This means that we use the communication style that we are most comfortable with, even though it may not be best for those who are listening to us.

Let us look at the different ways we should be communicating.

Sight or Sound?

There is a Chinese proverb that goes along the lines of, *"Tell me, I'll forget. Show me, I'll remember. Involve me, I'll understand."*

It is true, but only in the broadest sense. It does illustrate that people learn in different ways. Bear in mind that communication is teaching.

When introducing a new policy to your employees, you want them to learn it and put it into practice. You also want new suppliers to learn what your expectations are and make sure they meet them. To do this, you need to find out what someone's learning style is and make sure that you target it.

There is a communication myth that only 7% of understanding comes from the actual words that we use, 38% comes from the pitch pace volume and tone of voice and 55% comes from our body language and facial expressions.

This based on a misinterpreted study by Professor Albert Mehrabian in the mid 1990's. His studies pertained only to feelings and attitude when delivering a face to face message but was widely and wrongly taken to mean in all communication.

Try turning the sound off on the TV when the news is on, especially when there is no scrolling text or other picture cues. There is no way you will understand any item.

Listen to the world service news on BBC radio, where the presenters deliver almost everything in a pleasant monotone. You will undoubtedly understand every news item.

Try not to be taken in or absorbed by statistics on communication styles and effectiveness. Unless you understand the full context, the statistics are meaningless and are a guide, at best.

It is however important to note that people learn in three ways: auditory, visual and kinaesthetic. This equates to the Chinese proverb that I started with.

"Tell me, I'll forget. Show me, I'll remember. Involve me, I'll understand."

If you simply deliver your message in a flat monotone, if it is a simple and straightforward message, most people will get it. They may not engage with your message, so you may not achieve the desired results.

When you deliver a message and modulate your voice a bit, speed up and slow down and have a few changes of volume, you become much more interesting, cause engagement with the message and are more likely to get the desired results.

Auditory learners will be more engaged with the message than visual or kinaesthetic learners will.

If you introduce a visual component to your message (perhaps the much-maligned slide presentation of which there will be more information later), then those with a visual learning style will become more engaged.

To get a full connection with the kinaesthetic style learners, ideally you need to involve them in some sort of physical activity.

If, for example, you are introducing a new bonus scheme, you could start by telling people the basic outline of it with enough detail for the auditory learners to grasp it. You could then present the full detail pictorially, either in a hand out or on a slide. This would get the attention of the visual learners as well. Finally, instead of doing the normal thing and showing illustrations of how much bonus will be paid, give people a work sheet and get them to work out the examples. This will engage the kinaesthetic learners as well.

Appeal to all

Research suggests that people are divided roughly equally across the three categories of auditory, visual and kinaesthetic. You need to try and appeal to all 3 groups; however, no one is solely in any one category, and appealing to all three styles will massively improve your results and engage people with your message.

It is not always possible to use handouts, slide shows or other visual aids, and in many meetings having people working on physical exercises can be awkward and even lead to difficulties in keeping control of the meeting.

If your only option is the spoken word, make sure that you still engage with each type of person in a group.

Research in the field of NLP (Neuro Linguistic Programming) has shown that people will engage better with you if you at least use their preferred language styles.

I am mostly an auditory learner. At some point in this book I will use, or have already used, the phrase "as I said earlier" or something similar. Even though I use the written word, my main learning (and speaking) style comes through.

You can take advantage of this by introducing the correct mix of words into your presentations.

For the auditory learners in your audience use words like *say, speak, talk, tone, listen, dialogue, quiet, loud, whisper* and *hear.*

For the visual learners, words like *look, see, imagine, focus, picture, sight, vision, bright, dull* and *colour* will get them engaged.

The scope for kinaesthetic learners is even greater and includes words like *touch, lift, push, pull, throw, brush, rough* and *smooth*; basically any type of tactile word will work with this group.

For completeness, I will mention two other groups that are seldom included in learning styles, but have been researched as sensory types in NLP (Neuro Linguistic Programming). These are olfactory (smell) and gustatory (taste).

These factors do not play a huge part in learning styles, but using words like *scent, aroma, sweet* or *juicy* might sway an occasional person to your way of thinking or increase people's engagement by a small percentage. It certainly will not do any harm.

Going back to the example of the new bonus scheme, you might want to say something like.

*"I suspect you have all **heard** (auditory) that we are introducing a new bonus scheme. Let's take a **look** (visual) at some of the **solid** (kinaesthetic) facts behind it"*

This sounds like a perfectly natural statement and will engage everyone in a group no matter what style they have and, as I wrote earlier, will have extra appeal for everyone, as no one is solely one type or another.

In the past few paragraphs, I have been writing about communicating a message to a group. It is even more important to be aware of the different styles when addressing individuals. While everyone does have a mix of learning styles, everyone has a major or preferred style.

If you listen closely to what the other person is saying, you will start to hear more words of one type or another, and this will tell you whether they are auditory, visual or kinaesthetic.

Once you have figured out their style, simply start using words that reflect it. This is not an easy skill to master. After all, you have a message to get across, and you need to be focused on the content of the conversation. This will always be your prime concern.

Your goal is to get your message understood and into the subconscious of the recipient. Using the right sensory language makes a huge difference, and it is worth making the effort to listen actively and adjust your style in order to better influence the listener.

Rhetorical devices

Most of us are brought up to make good use of our native language in every day conversation. At school, we are taught good grammar and sentence construction. These tools are all we need to be a good communicator or presenter.

If we want to influence people and get our message into their subconscious mind, then we need to employ better tools. Rhetorical devices are those tools. They are designed to make sure that your words have the maximum possible impact on the listener.
One of my favourites is the rhetorical question. In simple terms, it is asking a question to which you do not expect to receive an answer. It is especially powerful as an opening gambit where you want to connect people with your idea quickly.

Opening your board meeting with *"Where do you think the company will be in 10 years' time?"* is a nice rhetorical question. Everyone knows they should already have thought of the answer, and they will immediately start searching their brains for the answer. While they do this, they will not be answering you, but they will be opening up all the correct areas of the brain into which you will feed the answer.

Another favourite of mine is alliteration, starting consecutive words with the same letter. *"Our marketing team is made up of colourful, creative characters."* This works best in threes as it also introduces a sort of melody to the words. The words do not need to be exactly consecutive. It is ok to introduce a conjunction between one or more of the words.

To continue from the rhetorical question above, you might say "Now is the time to make the business blossom and bloom so that we will be the market leader in ten years' time."

Perhaps the most powerful rule of all is the rule of three. There is an old Latin phrase "omne trium perfectum" which means everything that comes in threes is perfect. One of the greatest philosophers of the old world, Aristotle, even mentions the rule of three in his book on rhetoric. As with alliteration, the rule of three sets up a rhythm, which our brain likes and therefore connects with.

Children's literature exposes us to the rule of three at an early age and continues throughout our lives.

We get the three bears, three billy goats gruff, and the three little pigs. Even if you have never seen the movies, you will likely be aware of such classics as *The Good, the Bad, and the Ugly* and *Sex Lies and Videotape.*

Most adults will instantly complete the phrase "A Mars a day helps you…." The rule of three was used by their marketing team to produce one of the most memorable slogans of the late 20th century. The fact that "work, rest and play" rhymed with "a Mars a day" helped a lot as well, but for business communication, poetry tends to sound a little twee.

The rule of three pervades world history. Even the flags of many nations have three colours. The French national motto is Liberté, Égalité, Fraternité (Liberty, Equality, Fraternity). When Julius Caesar arrived in Britain, he is supposed to have said Veni, Vidi, Vici (I came, I saw, I conquered). In Shakespeare's Julius Caesar, Mark Anthony says "Friends, Romans, Countrymen."

We may forget some facts, figures and dates from our school lessons, but due to the use of rhetorical devices like the rule of three, some things are never forgotten. Use these in your communications, and they will be remembered.

There are many more rhetorical devices, but unless you are in politics or are promoting a worthy cause, the few I have mentioned, along with some similes and metaphors, are sufficient for getting business messages across in an interesting, colourful and memorable fashion.

Many people get confused about the difference between similes and metaphors; personally I don't think the difference is important. A metaphor states that one thing is another. "Life is a roller coaster."

"My college professor is a dinosaur." A simile states that one thing is like another. "Her eyes were like saucers." "I can swim like a fish."

Metaphors in business are somewhat more powerful than similes because they make a bold statement.

"Time is money" and *"knowledge is power"* are two of the best known business metaphors. Because of their simplicity and directness, they are known to almost everyone in business.

Similes are great for the softer, more fun items. If you are introducing a new commission structure for your sales force and want to get them on board, just tell them when they hear the detail they will feel as if they have won the lottery. If you use this one, make sure it is a good commission structure.

Modelling greatness

We cannot all be good at everything, but we can be good at anything. Being good at something is a choice. With few exceptions, due to illness or injury, we humans can achieve just about anything.

World champion athletes are not born champions. They train to be champions. The same can be said of musicians and actors.

There are a few people who seem to have a natural talent for high achievement, but for most people, it is a conscious decision, followed by a lot of hard work.

The greatest performers in any field tend to make their decisions at a young age and then immerse themselves in their chosen field. The younger this process starts the better.

In his bestselling book *Outliers: The Story of Success,* Malcolm Gladwell makes repeated reference to taking ten years or 10,000 hours to become an expert. Other researchers have carried out similar studies and agree that these figures are accurate.

I took up public speaking late in life. I was in my early forties. I was also unaware of the research relating to ten years or 10,000 hours to become an expert. Ten years after I started my public speaking career, I became the UK Public Speaking Champion and have since won several UK and international championships. I regularly compete against the same people, most of whom have been competing for ten or more years.

Every so often, a shining star arrives on the scene and lights up the competitions with raw, natural talent. Occasionally, they win, but more often than not, they manage to achieve a 2nd or 3rd place and then fade away.

The reason for this is that they have not studied the subtle nuances of speech that impresses audiences and judges, and they have not served the ten-year apprenticeship that helps them keep going when times get tough.

The exceptions to this ten year/10,000 hour rule are the competitors who get themselves a coach and mentor. They learn from people who have already achieved what they want to achieve and can steer them away from the pitfalls and towards best practice.

I did not even think about a coach or mentor during my journey from nowhere to the top; hence it took me the full ten years. As a professional speaker, coach and trainer, I now have a coach of my own, to make sure I am constantly progressing and developing. This stops me wasting my time learning stuff that someone can show me quickly.

If you want to improve your business through better communications, then you should consider getting a coach or mentor and learning directly from them. If you do not feel that a coach or mentor is right for you, and many people don't, despite the evidence that shows it is the fastest way to the top, then the internet is your coach.

Sites like YouTube, Vimeo and ted.com are awash with great speakers displaying amazing talent.

Don't just look at the business speakers; look at the entertainers and the politicians as well. Politicians are especially good at getting people to buy into their message. Mahatma Ghandi, Winston Churchill, Martin Luther King and John F Kennedy, were all amazing orators, and it is worth studying their speeches.

Each of these speakers have left a lasting mark on their societies because of their skill, not only in speaking, but in the construction of the speech they delivered.

Each of these speakers also left us with memorable quotes that are almost instantly recognisable, often to people who were not even alive when the speech was given.

"They may well have my dead body, but not my obedience." – Mahatma Ghandi 1925
"We will fight them on the beaches" – Winston Churchill 1940
"Ask not what your country can do for you" John F Kennedy 1961
"I have a dream" - Martin Luther King 1963

I wasn't alive when two of those speeches were made, and I wasn't even a teenager when the other two were given, but I am at least aware of them and the changes in society that were brought about by the catalytic reaction to those speeches.

When it comes to business speakers, check out the speech by Steve Jobs where he introduces the iPod and the speech on ted.com by Simon Sinek where he talks about why people buy from you.

Chapter 3 Summary

In the wrap for this chapter, I first ask you to think not just about your communications but also about your business and its sustainability. Is your business constantly changing and developing to meet a changing market? Is your business structured in a way that allows it to be adaptable? Is your business going to be your legacy and still be around in 200 years' time?

Are you actively watching communications from your competitors? Are you communicating changes in your market to your employees at all levels of your business? Are you listening closely to their responses?

"Tell me, I'll forget. Show me, I'll remember. Involve me, I'll understand."

Are you using visual, audio and kinaesthetic communications when listening as well as when speaking or writing? Have you thought about the words that you use and what type of communicator you are?

Do you use all three types of language when talking to a group, but focus on the listener's style when communication is one to one?

Are you introducing good rhetorical devices into your communications? Are you thinking about the rhythm of your words as well as the content? Are you using rhetorical questions to open with, in order to engage people's brains in the right gear from the start? Are you checking out great speeches and great speakers on line in order to see what fantastic one to many communication looks like?

Your job as a communicator is to influence people and get them to come around to your way of thinking. By using the tools mentioned in this chapter, you will be a lot nearer to that goal. Using these techniques is not manipulation. It is a short cut to achieving your goals.

Never lose sight of your objective, which is to have a profitable business that is going to survive long after you retire. Using great techniques for great communication will achieve just that.

Do remember and keep listening and checking that people are on message. If they are not, check whether the message is right or if the issue is with the delivery and adjust whichever is causing the problem.

Chapter 4 Connect With Stories

The writing on the wall

Scientists and researchers cannot agree when humans first developed speech. Estimates vary massively and range from 2 million years ago to 50,000 years ago.

Whenever it started, it was a massive leap forward in the way we communicated and developed intelligence. Prior to the evolutionary step of speech, humans communicated with grunt like sounds and gestures in the same way that animals do today.

Grunts and gestures can communicate a great deal of information but cannot express complex ideas as they lack the syntax required for sophisticated communication.

Sounds and gestures for "danger," "safe," "food," "water," etc. were probably commonplace and allowed humans to share some ideas about their immediate surroundings. There were probably sounds and signs for "near," "far" and "very far." Trying to communicate the idea that food and water could be found in a three days' walk to the south, but to avoid the mud after the fourth stand of trees was probably impossible.

The development of language changed all this and allowed not just sophisticated communication, but also the concept of discussion and the sharing of ideas.

It also let people recount the events of their day or their journey. Initially, this would have been simple and practical but through time would have been embellished, initially to fill in forgotten details and later to make it seem more exciting. With this came the art of storytelling.

I have a vision of the hunters sitting round the fire at night telling tales of close escapes, how they spent all day stalking a fierce animal before overcoming it and bringing it back to feed the tribe. This story would likely include details about how they came from downwind to avoid the animal sensing them and how they got the spear in the right place to stop and kill it.

The story had multiple purposes: to teach the young how to hunt, to entertain the tribe and to make themselves look good.

There is still disagreement about cave paintings and their purposes. I side with those that think they were drawn as part of the story and depicted scenes from the hunt. These scenes would be a lasting memory of the type of animal hunted and may even have had clues to the location of the herds that were they prey of our forebears.

Whatever the true origins of the cave paintings, they were the first attempts at human communication by a means other than writing or gesture. They were also the first form of permanent recording.

Human memory is subject to failure. Research suggests that it is seldom 100% accurate. We see and experience things and then interpret them in whatever way best fits with our normal view of the world.

Recording a message in a permanent form reduces the chance of misinterpretation by others. Most of the early cave paintings appear to depict a prey animal or group of animals often being hunted. This presumably indicates to those who have not yet seen them what they should expect when it is their turn to hunt.

Perhaps different caves had different animals painted on them to depict what should be found when the tribe's roaming brought them back to that location. Whatever the reason, and we will never know for sure, it is almost certain that the picture was an adjunct to a story.

As I said earlier, these pictures were the first form of permanent recording. The earliest paintings are estimated to be around 40,000 years old and were of course rudimentary. Later pictures became more sophisticated and, as well as animals, they often depicted hunting scenes, showing hunters with bows, spears and axes.

It took a further 30,000 years to move from painting to writing as a means of recording information permanently. By this time, human speech was extremely advanced, had enabled people to settle permanently, interact with other groups and conduct trade.

Some of the earliest texts were given as stories. "The Instructions of Shuruppak" is one of the earliest known written texts. It comes from Sumerian culture around 2,600 BC and is a set of instructions for good communal living. It is written as a story told by the king to his son.

Egyptian hieroglyphs on the pyramids are written as stories, relating to how the Pharaoh will make his journey into the afterlife.

Stand on the shoulder of giants

You can see from the previous section that human society, language, symbolism (painting and drawing) and writing all developed together. Without these skills, we would still be living a precarious existence in the Stone Age.

The ability to pass information from one generation to another through verbal and written stories has made a huge difference to our societies. Theatre, cinema, radio and TV are almost 100% dependant on stories for their existence.

Isaac Newton is quoted as saying, *"If I have seen further than others, it is by standing upon the shoulders of giants."*

Of course, like many quotes, he was paraphrasing what someone else once said. The earliest version of this quote was around 1100 AD by the French philosopher Bernard of Chartres who reportedly said, *"We see more and farther than our predecessors, not because we have keener vision or greater height, but because we are lifted up and borne aloft on their gigantic stature"*

The sentiment of this quote is that we can achieve more by building on the work of our predecessors than we can by starting from a blank slate, and so it is with stories.

There is no need to create stories out of nothing. Most of your stories can be created from your own life experiences and embellished a little to help make a point.

It is important that you do only embellish or exaggerate your stories. If your stories are complete fabrications, people will see through them, as they probably will not match your character, or there will be inconsistencies with the details.

Writers of fiction have been using scene setting and description since the first novel was printed *(Le Morte d'Arthur by Thomas Malory, published 1485).*

When we read fiction, it is important for us to be able to picture the characters and imagine the setting in which events play out. This allows the story to gel with our experiences and access our subconscious to make it seem more real.

When telling your stories, you need to stand on the shoulders of the literary giants that came before us and make your stories as real as possible to your audience.

When you have a story that might help to make a good business point, make sure you give it plenty of colour and add a bit of atmosphere. Place it in a specific time, and give the characters a bit of life by describing them. Describe a little of the scenery round about. Were you indoors or outdoors? Was it dark? Was it light?

Always remember that you are not writing a novel or telling a folk tale around a campfire. You are trying to make a business point. Atmosphere and descriptions are important, but do not let your message get lost in the telling.

My first boss was quite small looked gentle and had a mop of sandy coloured hair. He was however prone to fits of rage and flew into fits of temper without warning. I once described him as looking like a cute little teddy bear with the roar of a grizzly bear.

The latter description is a lot more interesting and good enough for a quick story about looks being deceptive.

My own story about how I got started in public speaking is quite dull, but with a bit of atmosphere, description and dialogue I make it quite interesting for those who attend my seminars and workshops.

It goes like this.

It was a warm humid evening in 1991, I was in a large, stuffy, dully lit basement room making my first ever presentation using PowerPoint software.

My audience were all members of the institute of master builders, a tough crowd. It was my job to convince them to sign up for an appointment with one of our sales team with a view to buying some training in Microsoft Office.

I felt that my presentation was going well as everyone appeared attentive. I sensed rather than heard the rear door of the room open. I glanced up and saw my boss's large frame duck through the door, straighten up and slide along the wall.

Despite a feeling of dread at his presence, I continued with my demonstrations. At the end of the evening, over 75% of the delegates signed up for a sales visit.

The next morning, I was still feeling quite smug and basking in my success when Frank walked into my office. He loomed over me, fixed me with his piercing grey eyes and asked, "How do you think last night went?"

"Brilliant," I replied, "We have 95 people interested in appointments."

"Not good enough," he yelled. "If your presentation skills were half decent, you could have signed everyone up" and walked out of the office.

I did not argue; there was never any point in arguing with Frank. Although he had not said anything specific, I knew that if I did not improve both my presentations skills and my sign up rate, things would not end well for me.

Ironically, although I worked for a training company, there was no budget for training. I mentioned my predicament to a more senior and successful colleague, and he agreed to mentor me.

With Peter's guidance, my presentation skills improved, and my sign up rates increased. My confidence grew as well. Peter encouraged me to invest in some training and to study in my spare time. My skills, confidence and sign up rates grew further. Even when Peter left the company, he continued to mentor me and point me in the right direction.

Nothing was ever good enough for Frank though, and I soon followed a stream of others and moved on to pastures new. Without his bullying and Peter's guidance, I would not be where I am now, so it was not all bad.

That story takes about three minutes to tell and is a useful way for me to let people know how I started out and that I used training and mentoring to get where I am; I didn't make it all up, and I did indeed see further by standing on the shoulders of giants.

The Hero's journey

The little story that I wrote above is a limited example of a literary device called "The Hero's Journey," also known as the monomyth.

The hero's journey was first described by Joseph Campbell in his 1949 book *The Hero with a Thousand Faces*

Campbell studied hundreds of myths and tales from around the world and said that most myths and tales can be boiled down to the following statement.

"A hero ventures forth from the world of common day into a region of supernatural wonder: fabulous forces are there encountered and a decisive victory is won: the hero comes back from this mysterious adventure with the power to bestow boons on his fellow man."

The story of Jason and the Golden Fleece, which is about 3,000 years old, conforms to the hero's journey and is undoubtedly one of the texts that Campbell would have studied. J.R.R. Tolkien's *The Hobbit,* which was written about 12 years before Campbell published his book, is another fine example of a hero's journey.

Since the publication of *The Hero with a Thousand Faces*, the writers of many books and films have openly said that they referenced Campbell's work while plotting their stories. These include Arthur C Clarke's "2001 a Space Odyssey" and George Lucas's "Star Wars."

Campbell broke the Hero's Journey down into three stages or "acts." Each act has multiple sub divisions, but discussing them in detail is beyond the scope of this book and not all of them apply to every hero's journey.

In act 1, or "departure," the hero is living a normal life when some event disturbs their life and sends them off on a quest that is beyond their current ability and often takes them into a sphere of which they have no knowledge.

In *The Lord of the Rings*, Frodo agrees to take the magic ring to destroy it in mount thunder, even though he has lived all his life in the peaceful sedentary land of the shire and has no knowledge of the world outside.

The hero is usually reluctant at first but meets with a guide or mentor; in Frodo's case, it is the Wizard, Gandalf, who persuades Frodo to set off on the journey by convincing him that deep down he does have the skills to accomplish the task.

Sometimes the hero initially refuses to accept the task but is always persuaded by the guide or mentor to take up the burden. The final part of act 1 is where the hero crosses the threshold from their comfortable world into the unknown and begins the journey.

In act 2, or "initiation," the hero meets with various tests and trials along the way. These trials are eventually met and conquered, sometimes alone but often with the aid of a helpful stranger or by their guide putting in an unexpected appearance and helping when things are at their toughest.

There are still failures along the way, and the hero often needs to do some deep soul searching before getting back on the right track again. Ultimately, the hero will reach their goal when they achieve the object of the quest along with an understanding of self-fulfilment.

There is then a period of rest and reflection before the beginning of the final act.

In act 3, or "the return," The hero sets out to go back to their everyday life while still in possession of the object of the quest. In many myths like Jason and the Golden Fleece, this is a physical object. In others, it may be an increase in status (the common hero becomes a prince or princess).

The journey back may well be as fraught as the outward journey and may need the guide or mentor to step in, but more often, the ordinary person who set out makes it back on his own as a conquering hero.

When the hero returns, they often become leaders amongst their people and share the knowledge and wisdom gained through their quest, and the benefit is therefore shared amongst many.

If you examine my story above, you will see that it has some elements of the hero's journey but not all.

My comfortable world was disturbed by a bullying boss, which caused me to set off on a journey to improve myself and perhaps prove myself to my boss. I found a mentor and with his help crossed over into a land of self-development and improvement.

I glossed over the hard work that was needed to get me to the desired standards; I did not mention the assignments that I had to repeat or the doubts that sometimes crept in. I actually save this for another story later in one of my presentations.

The important part is to show people that I did not do it all on my own and that I had to enlist help. People are less likely to follow your lead if you portray yourself as someone who can do everything without help. If you want to inspire people, you need to let them see that someone inspired you.

Most people see perfection as unattainable, and if you appear perfect, people will assume they can never be like you and won't follow your examples.

At the end of my story, I relate how, after training and mentoring, my skills improved and my performance was much better. I do not finish with the classical elevation, where I would be promoted, but it is not the end of the story.

Later in my presentation, I talk about how I changed jobs, moved up the ladder into senior management and began to mentor people, and this is where the story comes to a better conclusion.

When telling stories to illustrate a point or inspire your work force, make it personal and use the elements from the hero's journey. It has been proven in thousands of books and films.

It is an effective way of showing yourself as a leader who has faced challenges and overcame them with training and mentoring. This not only makes you look more human, but it also makes your staff more inclined to see you as a mentor or guide.

Folk tales

Many people think that folk tales are just for children, but in this section, I will ask you to reconsider that. Many folk tales were written not just to entertain children, but also to educate them, almost by stealth.

"The three little pigs" is a tale about both building on a strong foundation and learning from others' mistakes.

In the first part of the story, the first pig has his house of straw blown down by the wolf, and the second one learns from it and builds his out of stronger sticks. When this house is blown down, the third pig builds from brick. As the only tool the wolf has at his disposal is his "puff," the house is effectively indestructible.

There are multiple lessons in the first part of this tale.

1 You do not just fail once. You can fail multiple times and as long as you learn from the mistakes, you will eventually succeed.

2 If you learn from the mistakes of others, you will succeed earlier by avoiding them.

3 Using the correct materials will produce a strong building.

There is a second, often untold, part to the story. The wolf tries to trick the pig by telling him where to find a field of turnips and to be there at six in the morning. However, the pig gets there at five in the morning and is gone before the pig can catch and eat him. The wolf then tells him about where he can find apples, but the pig gets there early and tricks him again. The wolf tries one more time by telling the pig where he can find milk to make butter, but is yet again outsmarted by the pig arriving early.

This is a classic case of stubbornness and an unwillingness to change, even in the case of repeated failures. The mantra, "If you do what you've always done, you'll get what you've always got," is apt for this particular tale.

The tale then ends up with the wolf taking desperate measures, climbing down the chimney, presumably ignoring the danger signs of heat, smoke, and steam coming from the fire and cooking pot down below.

I am sure that if the wolf sat down and made some plans, he could have dug traps, set snares or even invented a bulldozer, but his inability to change finally led to his demise.

Cinderella, Snow White and Sleeping Beauty are all great stories about how evil people met their demise because they took inappropriate actions through jealousy. The people to whom they were nasty were all good people.

The outcome could have been so much better if they had worked with them in cooperation rather than resorting to underhanded tactics, which eventually became their undoing.

The story of the shoemaker and the elves is a tale about the good being rewarded,

As thanks for being good people who were down on their luck, the elves made shoes for the shoemaker and they were so good that the shoemaker commanded a higher price for them and became wealthy again.

It is also a tale about reciprocity as the shoemaker and his wife later make fine clothes for the elves as a reward for their assistance.

There are also modern, business related stories that could be considered folk tales.

My favourite one is about the businessman who sees the fisherman come in to his beach side property with his small boat and a few fish.

He asks the fisherman how long he had been out, and the angler replied "between two and three hours." The businessman said, "if you stayed out for eight hours you, could catch three times as many fish" to which the fisherman replied, "I don't need more fish. I have enough to feed my family and sell a few to pay for necessities and leave some over to go for a few drinks with my friends for an evening."

The businessman explains that he has a PhD and an MBA from Harvard. He would write a business plan showing how if the fisherman worked a few more hours he could make more money, buy a bigger boat and employ some help. He could then make even more money and buy another boat, then two, then three and then a whole fleet and eventually buy his own processing plant and become a millionaire.

The fisherman said "How long would that take?"

"About 30 years" said the businessman.

"Wow, that is a long time" the fisherman replied, "What would I do after that?" The fisherman responded.

The businessman replied, "You could retire to a house at the beach, get a little boat, do a little fishing, laze about in the afternoons, and go drinking with your friends in the evening"

"Just like I do now?" concluded the fisherman.

An excellent tale about if it's not broke don't fix it, or that your view isn't necessarily the same as everyone else's.

I am not suggesting that your business meetings become places where you sit around and tell stories or that fairy stories and folk tales are designed for the boardroom.

What I am suggesting is that these stories grew from a need to show examples in a simplified form and that it may be worth studying some of these tales and see what lessons can be applied to your business. You can then relate similar tales with the same message.

The beauty of the folk tales lies in their simplicity and as we have already seen, simplicity is often the best way to get your message across.

Parables

Parables are similar to metaphors but are an extended version that uses a short narrative to make a point, often of a moral or ethical nature.

They have been used for centuries to let teachers, guides and mentors enter into discussions about difficult situations.

They can be used in business situations to do exactly the same thing. If you have a seemingly insurmountable task, perhaps the story of the boy and the starfish could be used to spark a discussion.

A man walking along a beach saw a boy picking up starfish and throwing them into the sea. He asked the boy why he was doing this. The boy replied, "The tide is going out. If I don't throw them in, they'll dry up and die."

The man smiled patronisingly and said, "But, there are miles of beach and thousands of starfish on every mile. You can't possibly make a difference!" The boy smiled, bent down, picked up another starfish, and threw it into the sea.

"Well," he said, "I made a difference for that one."

This short piece can be used to show that while some actions may appear futile, they are in fact making a difference. The difference can be difficult for outsiders to see, but as long as the person taking action is making a difference, then they will remain motivated.

Another parable I like is one that is quoted as being a piece of ancient Cherokee wisdom, but versions of it appear in many cultures.

An old Cherokee is teaching his grandson about life. "A fight is going on inside me," he said to the boy. "It is a terrible fight and it is between two wolves. One is evil – he is anger, envy, sorrow, regret, greed, arrogance, self-pity, guilt, resentment, inferiority and lies. The other is good – he is joy, peace, love, hope, kindness, benevolence, empathy, generosity, truth, and compassion. The same fight is going on inside you – and inside every other person, too."

The grandson thought about it for a minute and then asked his grandfather, "Which wolf will win?"

The old Cherokee simply replied, "The one you feed."

This is a great example of demonstrating that whatever you focus on is what you get. It is a good story to get people in business to think about where they are applying their energy and the results it produces.

My final parable will appeal to everyone in sales, and I will leave you to draw your own conclusions about its meaning.

A salesperson, Brian, was upset at losing an important sale. In discussing the matter with his manager, Brian said. "I guess," he said, "It just proves you can lead a horse to water, but you cannot make him drink."

"Brian," said his manager, "let me give you a piece of advice, your job is not to make him drink. It's to make him thirsty."

Chapter 4 Summary

Telling stories does not always come naturally, and many business people are uncomfortable with the idea of standing up at a meeting and telling a story.

The powerful connection that is made to the subconscious through narrative is one of the fastest ways to get a message across.

Never underestimate the power of stories; our existence is probably due to the passing of knowledge through stories across the centuries.

We know a lot about how our forebears lived in the distant past through the stories that were passed along, initially verbally, then in pictures and finally in writing.

There is no need to re-invent the wheel when it comes to stories. The work has all been done by those who came before us.

It is up to you to use their techniques for colour, atmosphere, dialogue etc. to enhance your stories and bring them to life.

Folk tales and parables are great tools for opening up discussions and making a point. Do not be afraid that people will think you patronising them by retelling the story of the three little pigs.

The business lesson contained in that story is extremely powerful.

If you are brave enough to use it, then people will remember it and the message portrayed. Have a think about your childhood stories and see if any of them have a message that can be fitted to your business.

Use personal stories based on the hero's journey to show how you overcame adversity and succeeded when the odds were against you, but remember there must be someone helping the hero along the way as no-one likes a know it all.

When talking to prospective new customers, couch business successes in the form of a story. Make sure the outcome is not just your product or the bare facts of what you did. It needs to show what the extra value was for the customer and how they felt when you went the extra distance.

Stories connect; make sure you can connect with a story.

When I worked as an accounts trainer, one of my clients phoned up to say he had a problem processing bank payments. After a lengthy call, I determined that his modem was faulty. He was in a panic, as he needed to process payments for his clients before midnight. It was 4:00 pm, and he had no idea how to fix the issue.

Although he had not purchased his hardware from our company and we were trainers and not technicians, I decided to help. I went to a computer store, bought a new modem, drove to his house and installed it.

This customer was so delighted by that level of service, he consistently recommended us to everyone he did business with.

Use success stories like this to connect with future clients.

Chapter 5 Life With PowerPoint

Other brands are available

Pre-prepared presentations have come a long way since the use of overhead projectors and acetate sheets became popular in the 1950's. Although the technology had been around since about 1870, it was only when the US army saw its benefit, in classroom training, that it began to proliferate.

It beat the old system of "chalk and talk" by quite a distance. Among the benefits were:

1. Material could be prepared well before lessons.
2. Teachers and lecturers did not have to worry about illegible writing on blackboards.
3. Materials could be reused.
4. A presenter could display material while still facing the audience.

This was a real revolution in education and business, cutting out hundreds, even thousands of hours of work in many cases.

The biggest problem with this technology was the creation of the acetate sheets.

Most were crudely hand drawn and handwritten, negating one of the most important features of the technology.

Graphs had to be created by hand, using rulers and coloured markers. Text could be typed onto the acetates, but mistakes were expensive, as they could not be corrected.

It was possible to photocopy from paper to acetate. I recall trying this once. The photocopier was too hot, and the acetate evaporated inside, completely ruining the copier. Being an honest person, I did not answer when the engineer asked if anyone knew what had happened.

In the 1980's, the fledgling office software creators realised that there was scope for software to produce computer-generated presentations. One of the first, and for many years the market leader, was "Harvard Graphics." As well as the ability to write text onto computer generated slides and use built in cartoon style graphics, Harvard allowed users to import spreadsheet data and turn it into charts.

The pages created could be linked together and displayed in a sequence of "slides" on a computer screen. However, the graphics quality was poor, and the pages were often printed out to 35mm photographic slides, for use in a projector, hence the current naming convention.

The pages could also be printed onto acetates for use in an overhead projector. The results were not exceptional, but they served the purpose, and the software became popular.

A further leap in the technology occurred in the early 1990's. The graphical displays on computers got better, and LCD panels that could link to a computer and sit on top of the OHP became cheap enough for general use in schools, smaller colleges, training centres, and some small businesses.

At about the same time, the military, universities and larger corporations were beginning to use early versions of the data video projectors that we are all familiar with today.

Microsoft recognised the need to get into this market, and once they integrated PowerPoint into the Microsoft Office suite, the rest as they say is history.

PowerPoint has made such an impact that people often refer to giving a talk using presentation software as a PowerPoint slide show, even when they are using other software.

There are other presentation software packages out there.

Apple Mac users rarely use PowerPoint thanks to the "Keynote" software which users claim is simpler to use and gives a more elegant show.

"Prezi" is a free presentation software package that, at the time of writing in 2016, is gaining popularity in some quarters. One of its major features is that you can show your slides in any order, rather than the linear fashion of most packages.

Google has their own contender with "Google Slides." It has a simple user interface. It is not quite as flamboyant as some of the other packages, but many like it for this reason.

"Haiku Deck" is another free presentation package, which is gradually gaining ground, and users have described it as simple and elegant.

While doing some research for this section, I discovered that you can still buy Harvard graphics, in the US only, for $70.00. I doubt it will ever be a major contender, but it is good to know that the software that started it all is still hanging in there.

Simple is super

No matter which piece of software you decide to use in your presentation, the key is to "Keep it Simple."

I remember when I first started to use presentation software, I was so stunned by the features and the endless possibilities for impressing my audience that I got completely carried away.

Every slide change was done with a different transition. I had fades, wipes, checkerboards, reveals and anything else I could find.

There were bullet points sliding in from the left, right, top and bottom, appearing in place or bouncing round the screen.

My hard drive was full to bursting with clip art from magazine cover disks. I did not use same image twice.

The saddest thing about these presentations was that the audiences were validating them, and I was not noticing the lack of business impact.

I would stand up and present at least twice a week. As people were leaving, they said how impressed they were and congratulated me on the presentation. I became the go to guy for creating brilliant presentations.

I was not alone. Millions of people worldwide were using every bell and whistle available to give technically and artistically brilliant presentations. The message itself became less important than the delivery method.

Worse still, people, myself included, were spending more time working on the presentation than the data or message to be included. In 1997, I did a week's consultancy in a major international bank working with senior executives to prepare a presentation for the shareholders annual meeting.

There were 15 – 20 people involved at one point. There were lengthy discussions over fonts, transitions, colour schemes, chart types and a myriad of other minor topics. The presentation was a great success, but the cost in both time and money was probably not well spent.

This chapter is called "Life with PowerPoint" to contrast it with a phrase that became popular in the late 90's and is still heard regularly, "Death by PowerPoint." It took a long time, but eventually people became numb to all the bells and whistles.

There was a realisation, in some quarters, that the presentation was becoming more important than the message. People grew tired of going into meeting rooms and lecture theatres and sitting through fifty slides of often-meaningless information.

Even when the message was good and the information important, presentation software was being used to weaken rather than strengthen the message. Slides with complex information or lots of text would appear on the screen, and people would stop listening to the presenter and read the slide.

They would then try to catch up with what had been said and forget what they had read. The slide would advance, and the audience had not taken in either what was written on the slide or what the presenter said, even, as often happened, when the information was identical in both cases.

Sensory overload is a real phenomenon, and people's attention spans appear to be getting shorter. Unless you keep presentations simple and to the point, your audience will not get the message.

The answer is to start with your message and remember that at all times the message is key. When you do that, you will discover that if you keep it simple there can be Life with PowerPoint.

Start with the message

Starting with the message may seem blindingly obvious, but it is surprising how often the message is not as central to the presentation as it should be.

Let us say your objective is to address the staff at the end of the year and show how well the company is doing. You need to define, refine and evidence your message. "We are doing great, and next year is going to be better" is a great sentiment, but most people need to see something a bit more precise.

The message may end up as, *"Profits are up 10% from last year, and we expect a further 12% improvement next year. We achieved this through a mixture of trimming running costs and finding new clients. Next year, we expect to continue growing our client base and increasing the revenue from each client."*

If that is your message, then that is pretty much what you want to demonstrate with your slides. A bar chart showing three columns each bigger than the last will do the job well.

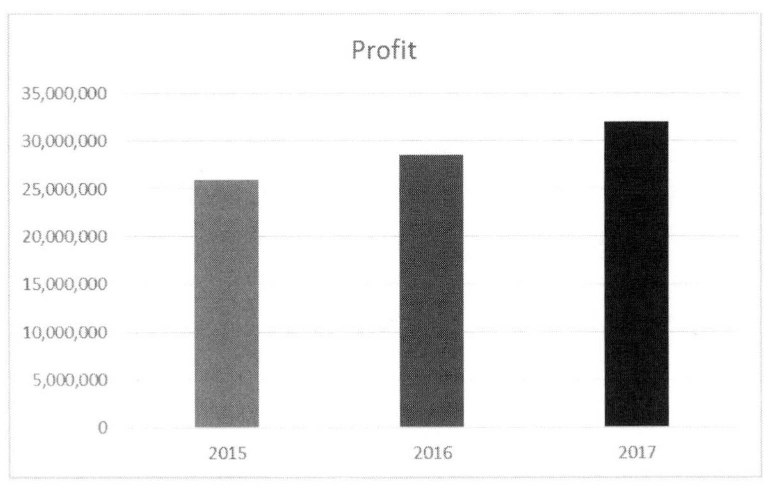

Instead of this, presenters will often display a spreadsheet showing actual figures and produce either a series of slides showing charts of revenue, costs and profit, or worse still a single chart showing all three.

Chances are the chart is going to look like a bit of a disaster as illustrated in the following diagram, but that does not seem to deter many presenters. They get bogged down in the act of creating the presentation and forget about both the message and the audience they are going to deliver it to.

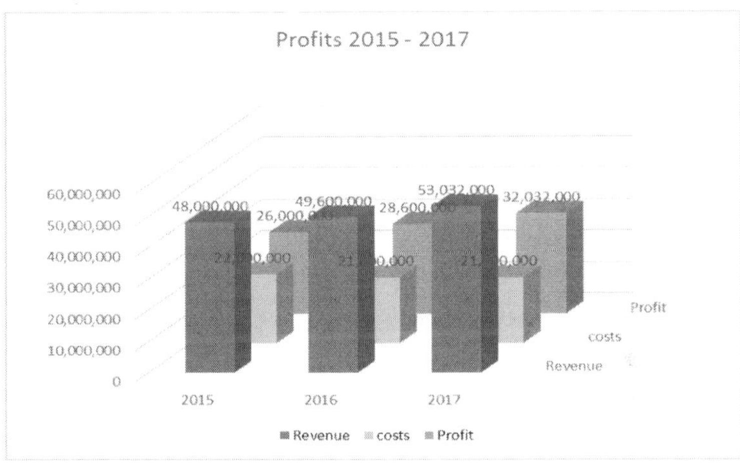

The data may be accurate. In full colour, a presenter may get lucky, and the chart will even look stunning if you ignore the figures overwriting the bars, but it is not the message they started out with.

The first chart shows the message that profits are up this year and will be up again next year. The presenter can explain that it was done by trimming costs and increasing customer revenues.

You may even have some more slides to show how you trimmed costs or increased revenues. If so, then that is another message, so define, refine and evidence each message in one simple slide.

You need one message on each slide so that the audience do not have to work hard to figure out the message. A simple slide also means that the audience will not be distracted trying to fathom it out while you are talking.

Of course, you want your slides to look good, so choose a pleasing colour scheme for your charts and a crisp clear font for any text. Make sure the font is big enough to be read from the back of the room. What looks good on your monitor may not be so pleasing projected from fifty feet away.

Anything that distracts the audience will detract from your message, which should always be your central theme.

A picture paints a thousand words

"A picture paints a thousand words" is a much used and often abused statement, but that does not mean it is not true.

A powerful picture will get to the heart of an idea much quicker and with more impact than simply describing the idea.

Think about a watching the sun set on the horizon as viewed from your hotel room window on your tropical island vacation. If you want to describe this, it could take some time.

There may be palm trees in the foreground and boats on the ocean. What colour is the sand? What colour is the sea? Are there some clouds? Are there any buildings? Producing a photograph will be more accurate, quicker and probably more powerful than most people could describe.

So it is with business. The first chart above paints a quick picture, and people see the upward trend instantly. Relating the bare facts and figures won't have the same impact or be so quickly understood. Whatever your message is, one slide with a simple picture on it can draw attention to the issue, and then you as the presenter can flesh it out with words.

If you want to get people to think about reducing expenditure, a picture of money flowing down a drain will make the point. If you are not recycling enough, a picture of a landfill site covered in rubbish should grab your audience's attention.

When you decide what message you want to make with a slide, write the message down. Writing helps access the subconscious, as you have to access different parts of the brain to write and think at the same time.

Once you have written the message, close your eyes and think of the most extreme outcome of your message. Once you have an image in mind, it should not be too difficult to find one.

Google will show you images for anything. Remember not to breach copyright. There are many copyright free pictures available.

If, for example, your business is going to be going through a period of slow but steady growth, and your message is that you want to make sure the progress is managed rather than rushing ahead with too much expansion at once. A google search will turn up thousands of images for "Tortoise and Hare."

Try to find images with impact or a degree of surprise. I recently coached a client who was giving a presentation on ethical investing for vegans, potentially a tough crowd, and we agreed on quite a surprising strategy. I got her to open with a graphic slide of animals in an abattoir.

This slide got the disapproving gasps that we expected, but once she made the opening statement "Is this how you want your money to be invested?", the audience was with her for the rest of a successful presentation.

A slide that is shocking is not for everyone. It is important to think about your audience. Can you risk something graphic? Will something funny go do down well? After you choose a picture, look at it and ask yourself, "Will this offend someone?"

The most important question is, "Does this picture enhance my message?"

When you move to a slide with a powerful image, do not speak immediately, pause for a few seconds, let people think about the image and then ask a rhetorical question. *"Are we the tortoise or the hare?"* Do not wait for an answer; move on with your presentation and explain your point. This is a powerful sequence and gets a message into the subconscious.

Remember: image, pause, question, explain.

Nothing to see here

Showing a picture and letting it rest on the screen for a few seconds before commenting is, as described, a great technique. Showing a picture while talking about something else is a disaster waiting to happen.

One of the biggest mistakes presenters make is leaving slides on the screen after they have finished talking about them. This can lead to the sensory overload mentioned earlier.

The brain does prefer visual information. If you leave a slide in place after you finish talking about it, a large portion of the audience will continue focusing on it after you start talking about the new message.

Remember, the rule is one slide, one message. If you have a slide with one message while talking about another, chances are neither message will be remembered.

There are lots of remote slide advance / pointers on the market. Hopefully, when you give a presentation, you use one of these rather than hitting keys on your laptop to advance the slide.

Many models now have a button, which will blank the screen so that when you have finished with a slide and do not want to show the next one, you can blank the screen.

Ideally, you will finish a message, advance the slide, and start your new message. This is not always possible. Sometimes you will use a slide to illustrate a point and then go on to tell a story relating to that point. You do not want anything on the screen at that time, so having a button to blank the screen is a great solution.

It is also useful to be able to blank the screen quickly if someone asks a question and you want the audience to be fully focused on you while you provide the answer.

Many presenters plan their slide show well, and when they know they will want to tell a story they show a “place marker” slide. This often has the presenter’s name and presentation title on it.

While this may seem like a good idea, people will still get distracted by the slide. If you are going to have a marker slide, make it blank and black so that nothing shows at all.

One of the features that I found useful when I started using presentation software was the ability to build a slide with bullet points. This was great for two reasons. It gave structure to the presentation, and I could use the bullet points as notes or prompts.

Most presentation experts now avoid bullet points for reasons related to the two points given.

Your presentation should be structured anyway. Bullet points are not needed to give the structure and often get in the way of it and dilute the message. I recall in my early days of presenting that I spent ages trying to find another bullet point because the slide looked too sparse.

Using bullet points as prompts generally means you do not have confidence in your ability to remember your presentation. The reality is you should not need to remember your presentation.

What you are doing is using a tool to enhance a message. As long as you know what that message is, you can stand up and present without any fear of forgetting. Your presentation will look so much more natural and pleasing that it will get to the subconscious of your audience and be remembered.

If you rely on bullet points as an aide memoire, then each time a bullet point appears, you will hesitate slightly, while you recall what you are going to say. Even the slightest break in flow will cause your audience to doubt you and your message.

When you are presenting a slide show from a platform or from the front of a room, chances are that the screen with your slides on will be centre stage. Make sure you think about your positioning so that you do not block the view of the slide or cast a shadow onto it.

People who are passionate about their message tend to become quite animated and will move from one side of a platform to the other while presenting. Done correctly, this can be powerful and engages the audience.

During a slide-based presentation, it can be distracting as the presenter passes in front of the screen. This is another case for using the "blank" button on the remote. A quick press before you hit centre stage and another as you have passed the screen, and it looks completely natural.

A word of warning: the remote advance/pointer is a wonderful tool, but when it has a blank button, mouse buttons, next slide, previous slide, page up, page down and a laser pointer button, you have a lot of potential for things going wrong. Make sure you get to know your tools before you use them.

Chapter 5 Summary

Before you start preparing your presentation, decide on the message. Everything you do from there on must be focused on the message.

A presentation should have one central message theme. There will be individual messages that relate to the main theme. Each slide should have one message and each individual message should have only one slide.

PowerPoint is not the only presentation software available. There are many alternatives, and as software goes online, there will be many more packages available.

Decide what features you need (and they are fewer than you may think), and choose the package that suits.

Every time you decide to use a feature, ask yourself if it detracts from the message or enhances it. If it does not enhance the message, then do not use the feature.

Try to run through your presentation and see how it looks in the actual environment in which it will be delivered. If that is not possible, make sure that your chart or graph takes up as much of the slide as possible.

Always get to your venue early in case you have to make some changes on the fly. Have the presentation on a memory stick as well as on your laptop. If you have a problem with your laptop, you may be able to borrow one and use your memory stick.

Many of the new presentation software packages are based online. This means that your presentation will also be online. If you are presenting away from your office, make sure you have guaranteed internet access in the venue.

Make sure you have an offline backup of your presentation and software to run it locally in the event that internet access is lost before or during your presentations, again going back to having your presentation in a memory stick.

Keep it simple. The days of showing off with presentations are over. Start with the message, stick with the message and finish with the message. Everything on the slides you have created should, in as simple and straightforward a manner as possible, enhance the audience's reception and storage of your message.

The brain prefers visuals, so make sure that your slides are visually pleasing. Words are important and contain the bulk of your message, so speak your words don't display them. Pictures make it easier for the brain to remember, as it will build an association.

When using presentation software, remember to master the tools so that you do not advance a slide when you meant to use the laser pointer or go to the previous slide instead of the next one.

Chapter 6 A Mission Or A Vision

Mission statement

Does your company have a mission statement? If you are part of a large corporate, it almost certainly will have one. Some smaller companies have mission statements as well, but many businesses neglect the mission statement.

Does your company have a vision statement? Most companies are not even aware of the vision statement or the need for it. Despite this, many of those companies have one, but it is wrapped up inside the mission statement.

What is the difference between a mission statement and a vision statement, and why should a company bother with both, or indeed either?

The mission statement is a statement about your company's purpose. It is about what you do and how you do it. It should set out standards of excellence and talk about how your business works in the present. The mission statement is how you communicate your message to everyone who comes into contact with your business.

The following is the mission statement (at the time of writing in 2016) of the Chubb Corporation.

"We are dedicated to providing excellent underwriting and loss control advice up front, and to ensuring superior customer service through the life of the policy. Our knowledgeable loss prevention experts can help commercial customers reduce losses in the workplace. Our personal appraisers are invaluable in determining accurate replacement value, which is more likely to provide you with the right amount of coverage for your valuable property."

This is an excellent example of a mission statement. It says that they are dedicated to excellence and superior customer service. It demonstrates that the staff are experts, and it acknowledges that the customers and their properties are at the forefront of their business.

It uses the word "are" in two key places to indicate that the mission statement is set in the present. In other words, "This is what we do right now."

When you develop a mission statement, make sure it answers the three key questions.

What do we do?
Who are our customers?
What makes us special?

The mission statement should be for the benefit of everyone that meets with your company. Shareholders, staff, customers and suppliers should all feel that your mission statement resonates with them.

It will probably be your staff that see the mission statement more than anyone else. Be especially careful to make sure that it resonates with them and has some mention of your company's expertise being due to the quality of those who work there.

It has been said the people's attention span is dropping in many areas and that we need brevity in all that we do. I have mentioned several times in this book that the easiest to assimilate messages are short and to the point.

I would make an exception in the case of the mission statement. Because it has to serve multiple purposes, it needs to have multiple parts. If you do want something short and snappy, you can do that with your company motto or slogan.

This is the mission statement of The Estee Lauder Company:

The guiding vision of The Estee Lauder Companies is "bringing the best to everyone we touch." By "the best," we mean the best products, the best people and the best ideas. These three pillars have been the hallmarks of our company since it was founded by Mrs. Estee Lauder in 1946. They remain the foundation upon which we continue to build our success today."

Part of that statement is also their motto, *"Bringing the best to everyone we touch."*

This is a particularly good mission statement because it talks about the products, the people and the ideas. They use "everyone" so that shareholders, staff, customers and suppliers can all feel that it is about them.

What is also good is that it uses the word vision at the start and then it goes on to mention that the mission statement is founded on the three pillars (a strong analogy) that were there at the beginning.

It gives a real impression of a company founded on one person's vision, and that that vision was maintained and eventually turned into the company's mission statement.

Vision statement

The vision statement is about looking to the future. What are the hopes and dreams for you and your business? It is about where you want to be and the values of the business. It should also be about why you are in business.

I doubt there are many successful businesses that were founded by someone without a vision. Most businesses are started because someone has a new idea or they have thought of a way to do something better than anyone else.

Bill Gates said in an interview, *“When Paul Allen and I started Microsoft over 30 years ago, we had big dreams about software. We had dreams about the impact it could have. We talked about a computer on every desk and in every home”*

Dreams do not come much bigger than that. Today, there are few desks that do not have a computer on them and few homes in the developed world that do not have a computer.

That vision has stayed with the company, and their current mission statement is, *“Our mission is to empower every person and every organization on the planet to achieve more.”*

To my mind, this is more of a vision statement than a mission statement. Although it is set in the present tense and encompasses everyone, it is too big for a mission statement but ideal for a vision statement.

Nike has a mission statement which reads, *"To bring inspiration and innovation to every athlete* in the world (* If you have a body, you are an athlete)."*

Starbucks’ mission statement says, *“To inspire and nurture the human spirit – one person, one cup and one neighbourhood at a time”*

Both of these are vision statements. They talk about inspiration, and although they give a sense of being present based, we know that as they are talking about reaching everyone that it is a long-term aim.

What is the mission statement for your company? What is its vision statement? Which should you deal with first?

The vision statement is probably the more important of the two. Your business probably would not have gotten started without a vision. It may have been a grand vision or it may have been a small vision, but it was enough to take action on and get started.

Maintaining this level of vision is what makes businesses grow. Few famous brands have one office or one outlet, and they grow not to make money, but because the people who run the company have a vision of being the biggest, the best or the worthiest.

If you want to grow, you can only do it if you first visualise it and impart that vision to everyone you come in contact with. You need to inspire your customers to buy from you. You need to inspire your staff to work for you and be happy doing it, and you need to inspire your suppliers to be proud to be associated with you.

It is important to have a mission statement that says what you do, who you do it for and what makes you different. It is even more important that you have your vision statement that communicates why you do it.

Ask yourself this one simple question and you will find the vision statement within the answer.

Why do I do what I do?

Departmental statements

Few companies have departmental vision or mission statements. Most businesses produce a mission or vision statement and expect that everyone in their company will work towards that end, no matter what part of the company they are attached to.

The reality is that most departments have their own culture, and while they seldom work actively against the company's goals, they often do not work towards them, as their departmental culture is the employees' driving force.

People relate more to their peers and to their team leaders than they do a senior manager who is three levels above them in the corporate structure.

For many employees, the company vision is something they hear about on their induction week and never even think about again.

Let us say that you have a training department within your organisation. Their role is to provide in-house training and to outsource courses that they are unable to provide. It is likely to be a small department with a close-knit group of staff.

They will be carrying out a repetitive process with a lot of the in-house training. The company will likely set them a goal to get everyone trained to a certain standard within a certain period. In fact, their own goal of making sure they score highly on the feedback forms, will probably drive them more than the company set goal.

Hopefully the two goals will mesh, but if they don't, it will be the departmental goal of getting good feedback scores that is likely to win out.

With the outsourced training, they may well feel budget driven and always go with the cheapest provider, based on the assumption that they are all delivering the same accreditation and must be the same standard.

Having been in the training industry at all levels for a number of years, these scenarios are all too familiar. I even know of trainers who "lost" evaluation forms in order to maintain their average scores.

If the training department had their own mission and/or vision statement to work with, it could be a different story altogether.

"The training department provides the highest quality of service to ensure that all employees are assessed and trained to the highest possible level of excellence."

Of course, the training department would need to be involved in the creation of this statement so that they are fully on board with working towards it. What about your customer service department or your operations department? Could they benefit with creating their own mission / vision statement?

What about the IT department? They often get a bad press and can be accused of being "Off message." IT is often much more structured than other professions, and it does attract a certain personality type. Many people in IT are not natural team players.

A week after I took a promotion from my training job to that of IT manager, the company mail server failed, and I discovered that it wasn't included in the data backup plan.

I did manage to rescue the server and get the data back. When I queried the departmental staff about why there was no email backup, they said there was no budget for the extra software. When I spoke to the MD, he told me that he had never been asked for a budget and things were done on an ad hoc basis.

It was not long before a budget was in place and the ad hoc nature of the department disappeared. We had a mission statement that said, *"The IT department will ensure that every system and every bit of data (pun intended) will always be fully functional and fully protected."*

By the end of my first year, we had a better relationship with the other departments, and the staff who used to be locked in their offices were often to be found in other departments chatting happily to their colleagues and resolving issues that previously might have been left until after office hours.

Departments need to work towards the goals and vision of the company as a whole, but it is still wise to have departmental statements that allow them their own culture as long as it aligns with that of the business.

Personal statements

As departmental statements are important to ensure that all departments are working towards the greater good of the company and keeping themselves aligned with the businesses message, it is important to ensure that individual employees also buy into the company culture.

It is absolutely vital that every employee has an individual action plan, that the employee is involved in the making of that plan and then sign off on, at the very least, a statement of intent.

The non-managerial employee is the last link in your chain, but is also the foundation on which your business will thrive or fail. These employees are the ones who produce your goods, organise your deliveries, talk to clients and, if not pulling in the same direction, set the tone of your workplace.

It is not good enough to pay lip service to the appraisal process; it has to be a genuine two-way appraisal with the employees feeding back to their team leaders and managers, as well as them receiving an annual critique.

Many organisations, and I have worked for some, have a culture of fear at appraisal time. Too often, the annual appraisal is linked to remuneration, and bosses give harsh appraisals in order to justify lower salary increments.

Employees go into these appraisals expecting to be told what their shortcomings are. They are therefore right to be concerned about the outcome. Most bosses will soften the blow by offering a bit of a praise and then launch into a list of issues that need to be improved.

In a situation like this, employees are likely to become either resentful or completely passive.

In the first case, they are liable to complain to their colleagues and cause a negative atmosphere in the workplace, which could affect their co-workers and lead to a department that is working against the company message.

They will also complain to their family and friends outside of the company. In extreme cases, I have heard employees openly complain to their customers, leaving the company's reputation in tatters.

In the second case, the employee will do the bare minimum to meet the appraisal targets and will probably work away quite quietly until they find another job and move on. If they have become passive, they won't even look for another job. They will sit at their desk underperforming until the next appraisal and eventually become resentful.

Employees who are genuinely involved in the appraisal process and can, within reason, negotiate their own targets and training are much more likely to be happy and contented at work. They may not go out and praise the company to everyone they meet, but they certainly will not be sabotaging its reputation.

Before an appraisal, both the employee and their manager should fill out their own appraisal sheets and exchange these a few days before the appraisal so that the communication begins at an early stage and there are no surprises during the appraisal.

The action plan should be created during the appraisal and not before it. This is especially important in situations where continuous accreditation is a job requirement.

At one company, my annual appraisal was held in what I felt were good circumstances. We had not exchanged appraisals beforehand, but there were open discussions. The appraisal felt fair, and my views seemed to be taken into account. I was therefore stunned when my manager pulled out an action plan and asked me to sign it.

The action plan included everything we had agreed on verbally. I felt manipulated and suspected my boss of steering me towards specific goals that suited the company rather than me. It was a good action plan, and one that was quite fair, but I found it hard to buy into it, as I hadn't been involved in its creation.

Had we filled in the action plan during the appraisal, we would probably have ended up with the same thing, but I would have been much happier because of my part in its construction.

Work with your employees, and let them have as much input to the action plan as possible. Use it to set out agreed goals that benefit both the company and the employee.

Leave a space at the end for the employees dream, what their vision is. Do they want to be an MD one day? If so, put it in their vision box, you never know; they might be the right person for the job.

Client or supplier statements

Your mission and vision statements should be global and aimed at everyone your business meets. This of course includes your suppliers and your customers.

Sometimes you need to go that little bit further with both your customers and your suppliers.

How will your customers be exposed to your mission or vision statement? They are not going to come looking for it. Hopefully you have given your statement(s) some kind of prominence on your web site. If you are the sort of business who goes out and pitches to clients, you will have included your statement(s) in your presentation and/or proposals.

You also need to keep reminding your customers why you are the best fit for them. It is seldom possible or even desirable to include your mission statement on every document that you send out. This is where a slogan can be useful.

Slogans like Nike's "Just do it" and Kit Kats "Have a break" are now so pervasive that you can't help but think of the brand when you hear the slogan even in isolation. They are also so short and snappy that they can fit on any document that they produce without taking up excess space or being obtrusive.

Do you have a slogan or motto? If so, do you put it on every customer communication? If you do not have one, it's worth considering.

A slogan or motto is a short, snappy statement that needs to be congruent with your mission and/or vision statement(s). Ideally, as with the Estee Lauder example above, it should be an excerpt from the mission/vision statement, but it's not necessary.

Keep it as short as you can. I suggest that ten words should be the maximum, or it risks being hard to remember. *"A Mars a Day helps you work rest and play"* is probably the longest slogan that I can remember. Even Pepsi's seemingly lengthy, *"Lipsmackin' thirstquenchin' acetastin' motivatin' goodbuzzin' cooltalkin' highwalkin' fastlivin' evergivin' coolfizzin',"* is only ten words, but I can't remember it all.

Your slogan should be easy to remember, and you should be comfortable with it. When I coach and consult, my goal is to make sure that my customer's message is remembered so my slogan is "making your message stick." In four words, this sums up what I do. I see this message dozens of times every day. It still resonates with me and reminds me what my duty to my customers is as well as letting them know what I am doing for them.

What about your suppliers? They are often coming from a somewhat different direction than other people you work for, and you need them to be working for you. It should not be a master and servant relationship; it should be more of a cooperative business model.

The message I send to suppliers is straightforward. *"If you want to work for me, work with me."* This fits the 10-word model for the slogan and gets to the point quickly.

If I am contacting a potential new supplier, that statement is included in all my communications. If you or your business issue invitations to tender, do you have a slogan that says something like *"We only work with great suppliers"?* In short, do your suppliers know instantly what level of service you expect?

Chapter 6 Summary

What is the state of your statements? Are they fit for purpose? If you are reading this book, then you are probably the type of person who has some good statements.

Do you review those statements regularly? If you have a vision statement, it should someday be realised, and then it will become the basis for your new mission statement. As you create a new mission statement, you will need a new vision statement. If your statements do not change, is it because your business has not grown?

There is a two-way process between statements and the entity to which they apply. If your business does not grow or your goals are not met, then your statement will not change. This is probably because there is a lack of congruence somewhere. In this circumstance, sometimes changing your statement to be more congruent can be the thing that helps you change and grow.

In business, everyone and everything needs a purpose. Creating an appropriate statement for your business, your departments, your staff, your customers and your suppliers will help clarify that purpose and align everyone to achieve the same ends.

Done right, this can even end up with your customers working for you.

The day before I completed this chapter, I gave a keynote speech on communication in my home city of Glasgow, Scotland.

Because of the relationship I built with those customers and the statements we shared, after the presentation, a large number of my customers were happy to stand in front of a video camera and give me a testimonial. Out of all the statements your business has, there is nothing better than a testimonial.

Chapter 7 Wizards And Warriors

The magic starts at the top

Few businesses get started without a vision. The tiny seed of a business idea probably appears in everyone's head at some time, and it probably happens to us all more than once.

The vast majority of these seeds will fall on stony ground and fail to germinate. Some seeds may be nurtured for a little while and begin to sprout, but the effort needed to produce a business may be too much.

Great business leaders are those who have a vision and nurture it all the way, until it becomes a thriving business.

Many entrepreneurs fail several times on their journey. Persistence, perseverance and learning from their mistakes, and those of others, is what gets them to the top.

Among the most prominent traits of great business leaders is the ability to hang on to their vision through their failures.

Henry Ford had dozens of jobs between leaving home as a young man of sixteen and setting up the Ford Motor Company at age forty.

Ford had two failed businesses behind him, but his vision, coupled with his powerful and passionate communication skills, enabled him to find fresh investors.

Richard Branson started his first business, "Student" magazine, at age sixteen. He also used that magazine to advertise cut-price records. From this success, he went on to open a record shop in London's Oxford Street. He almost lost his record stores after being accused of selling stock, which was marked for export only. His mother re-mortgaged the family home to help keep him afloat.

Over the years, dozens of business have been created under the Virgin brand. Many have failed, but Richard Branson has not only kept his vision going but constantly has new visions. He is currently working with another great visionary, Paull Allen, co-founder of Microsoft, to open up space tourism.

Like Henry Ford, Richard Branson and many other entrepreneurs are risk takers who believe in their vision and will do what it takes to make sure that their dreams end up as a reality.

Visionaries never stop dreaming. Once a dream is realised, they nurture the next seed of an idea and help it blossom into a business but are not downhearted for long if the idea withers and fails.

A great vision coupled with grit and determination is where most entrepreneurial journeys start. Sadly, it is also often, where the journey ends.

It is not enough to have a vision and start heading for the pot of gold at the rainbow's end.

Entrepreneurs need funding, and to get that funding, they need to be able to communicate their vision in a practical sense with a solid business plan.

The business plan needs to contain a description of your business in precise terms. It needs to start with a clearly written executive summary, which I would suggest you try to keep to less than 500 words.

The summary should be a clear synopsis of the business plan and lay out what funding you need and what you intend to do with the money. The detail comes in the rest of the plan.

The remainder of the plan should be as detailed and precise as possible. Many entrepreneurs fail because they cannot communicate the business plan successfully. They become blinded by the dream.

Investors want to know if you have done your market research, about the structure of your business, about your supply chain and what makes you different. Most of all, they need to know that their money is in safe hands and that in those hands it will be nurtured and grow into a substantially larger sum.

If you do not have the skillset to write a business plan, then you need either to learn it or seek assistance. Contact your local chamber of commerce; they often have contacts for organisations that help aspiring entrepreneurs with business plans.

There are many internet resources that have advice on writing business plans. Some will even sell you a template.

However you do it, you need to make your business plan clear, concise and business like; make sure you do not lose sight of the dream in the process.

The entrepreneurial journey is normally a two-step process. The idea germinates, and the entrepreneur runs with it and achieves a degree of success quickly. There is then a bit of a barrier as there is too much for one person to do.

I work in a shared office. On the wall opposite the desk I am using today, there is an unattributed quote that says, *"if you want to go fast, go alone. If you want to go far, go with others."* This sums up the entrepreneur journey rather neatly.

Who are the others?

What happens when going fast and alone has taken you to a point where you stop making progress and your business can't expand any further?

The danger at this stage is that your business may not just cease to grow, but it may start to shrink or even fail completely.

A good example of this are eBay sellers. Many people start selling goods on eBay on a part time basis and then realise that it is possible to turn it into a full time business. They purchase small amounts of stock, advertise on eBay, get some orders, pack the stock and send it off. The problem arises when they become successful at selling. Orders can begin to outstrip supply, or there is not enough time for one person to process the orders and get everything packed and shipped to the customer in good time.

Orders either are missed or delayed. This results in poor feedback, which is instantly obvious to prospective buyers, and a consequent down turn in business and revenue. The loss of revenue may lead to difficulties in purchasing new stock, which leads to more bad feedback. The business enters a downward spiral and eventually collapses.

A good entrepreneur will have spotted this coming and taken steps to avoid the issue or be prepared to resolve it when the time arrived.

The situation should have been envisaged early on and been part of the business plan. The problem with some businesses is that when capital is not required, a business plan is not made, as there is no one to communicate it to.

As well as being a means to attract investors, or secure a line of credit at the bank, the creation of the business plan should clarify our self-communication and makes sure that our internal dialogue is congruent with our business. Done successfully, the entrepreneur will recognise when it is time to seek outside help and "go with others."

Clearly, the type of business will determine what type of people "the others" are. If you plan to open a gourmet restaurant then you will need to employ a chef, some kitchen staff and some waiting staff from the outset. If you want to manufacture a physical product, you will need machine operators, packers, etc.

These will all have been accounted for in the initial business plan, even if that plan is a vague sense of where you are going and exists only in your head.

In those businesses, it is the other types of staff that you need to be thinking about. When is it time to stop doing your own marketing and employ someone? Are you still sitting down for five hours a week doing the payroll, are you banking the takings, sweeping the floors?

At some point, you need to stop working in your business and start working on your business. This is why you need to start employing other people. It can be difficult to let someone into your business and start working on your dream, but the reality is that it has to happen.

The business world is full of stories where business owners trusted people who then defrauded them or sabotaged the business, often by accident as they didn't care as much about someone else's business.

This is where planned growth is of vital importance. If you plan your growth, you will have a fair idea of when you need to employ someone else in your business. Make sure you start looking for someone well in advance of needing them.

The employment process should be different at the early stages of a business. Of course, you should ask for resumes, showing experience and qualifications. You should always check references and verify that letters of recommendation are genuine.

Beyond that, the most important thing is that you like the person you are going to be working with. A pre-interview coffee and a chat with prospective candidates in a relaxed setting will help determine if you are a good fit for each other. Once you have met a few people and decided which ones you feel comfortable with, then you can go for the more formal interview process.

It is important to do both in the early stages of a business.

In the relaxed situation, you will get a real feel for whether someone is genuine or not; if they do not appear relaxed, chances are they are holding back and not being completely genuine. If you do not feel 100% happy with the first employee in your business, you will never be able to trust them to work on their own.

The formal interview lets you ask the awkward testing questions. What is the biggest challenge you have resolved? What was your biggest failure? How did you recover from the failure? Do you expect to fail again? And so on.

The informal interview lets applicants see the human side of you and decide if the relationship will work or not. The formal process also lets you demonstrate that while you are looking for someone who is a potential friend and ally, it is you who is ultimately in charge.

The personal touch is necessary in the early days of growing your staff. It achieves two things. It makes sure that you gel with those you are working with and that they are your type of people.

It also helps ensure that your business will continue to employ the right type of person, as you are setting a culture that you hope to continue long after you can no longer be involved in the choice of employees.

The people that you employ are your ground troops, the warriors mentioned in the chapter title. If you choose them wisely and get them to buy into your vision, they will happily fight your battles without question as they will be fighting for the same cause.

The Middlemen

In the early days of an entrepreneurial business, you will have a strange army. Hopefully it will be an army that works for you.

There will be one general (you) and many foot soldiers. If your recruitment strategy has worked, these will be people that believe in your business and want to help you achieve your vision. What you will have will be more like a revolutionary mob than an army.

After a while, this is likely to become unwieldy and difficult to work with. Your business will be exciting and energetic, but there is a chance that the practical aspects will be neglected. People chasing a dream, even someone else's dream, are probably not the sort of people that want to get bogged down in the mundane world of paperwork, reports and statistics.

This is where you need to make some tough choices. Do you bring in a manager from outside to organise your foot soldiers, or do you promote from within?

If you bring in a lieutenant from outside, they may well get your troops organised and pulled together, but there are two big risks.

The first is good, old-fashioned jealousy. There is bound to be at least one person in the organisation that feels they were deserving of a promotion and will resent being passed over. They may well feel that your unspoken communication to them is that they are unwanted and not good enough. They might leave, and you lose a valuable asset.

Even worse, they may stay and become an issue for you, by working to their own disgruntled agenda.

This can create a bad atmosphere within the business, and this will be communicated to everyone who meets your disgruntled employee. If you have more than one resentful employee because you parachuted someone in from outside, you may well have a disaster in the making.

The second problem with bringing someone in from the outside is getting him or her to fit with your company culture. Up to this point, you have been living the dream and working towards your vision. You have brought people on board that you like and have come to trust, but now you are probably employing a more practical person who is not quite as connected to your dream.

They could stifle your existing work force in their attempts to bring order from the chaos that has been created in the fulfilment of stage one of your vision. If those people are no longer chasing your dream with the same vigour as before, then your plans could be delayed or destroyed.

Elevating someone from within has similar risks. Whom do you promote? Presumably you hired a bunch of capable workers. If you promote one, will the others became jealous and resentful? Will someone who has been more of a visionary have the practical skillset required to manage people? How easy is it going to be to replace that person's skillset, bearing in mind that whomever you promote will be taking a critical look at whoever takes on their old role?

It is a tough choice, and there is no simple or straightforward answers. Whatever you decide make sure you are looking at the desired outcome for you and your business.

Of course, we do not want to hurt or upset employees who may well have become our friends. The important thing to remember is that it is your company and your vision.

Whatever choice you make, the damage can be alleviated by good communication. Talk to your workforce at the earliest possible opportunity and let them know when a change is about to be made.

You may even be surprised at the outcome.

I once worked at a company where a redundancy in the sales support team had become necessary. At the board meeting where the decision was made, I managed to persuade the CEO and the sales director to go for a managed exit rather than the traditional, "clear your desk and go" approach.

The employee selected for redundancy was asked to a meeting and informed of the decision. There was then a team meeting to explain to his colleagues why the redundancy was necessary and the reasons why that particular employee was chosen.

Everyone was understandably upset, and the week ended on a low note. However, the following week ended on an extreme high when one of the sales support team presented the sales director with a fully prepared and workable plan.

Everyone in the team agreed to a sizeable cut in basic pay, so that the company wage bill remained the same. They would then make up the difference by running extra campaigns, which were outside their current remit, to generate more leads for the sales team, and they would get productivity bonuses.

Had we simply made someone redundant without a clear and open discussion, we would have lost a valuable employee and missed an opportunity for increased sales. The employee who mooted the plan to the group was not the employee about to be made redundant. She eventually rose through the ranks to become sales manager.

Succession planning

The reason that Helen from the sales support team eventually became sales manager was not due to her altruism, her organisational ability, her critical thinking or her personality. It was due to all of these and to a system that recognised the importance of succession planning.

The CEO had always insisted that no one in the business would be promoted unless there was someone there and ready to take his or her place. He made it clear that his preference was to promote from within wherever possible. Only basic grade employees should be recruited from outside, and even then people were encouraged to change departments at an early stage if it was thought to be a good fit.

Succession planning is extremely important, and it is essential to communicate this to everyone in an organisation. Knowing that there is a route to the highest level within a business and that you can only get to the top if you do your bit for those further down the ladder is a great motivator, not only to mentor someone to take on your role, but also to accept someone higher up the corporate ladder as your own mentor.

Coaching, guiding and mentoring are probably the most powerful tools available in succession planning. Training and qualifications have a big part to play in senior employee selection, but it should never be seen as the only factor.

In some industries, there are mandatory requirements for certification and accreditation. In some industries, it is essential for employees to be certificated in order for the business to remain accredited. These are great reasons for maintaining a training programme but should never be used as the sole basis for promotions.

The most important factor in employee advancement should be if they are the correct fit for the role. An employee needs to be aligned to the company's mission and vision. This only happens when they have been correctly mentored by someone else with the same point of view.

A properly mentored employee will also mentor their successor. They will ensure the person they choose to succeed them will be aligned to the company goals and be prepared to mentor their successor in turn.

When a good mentoring structure is in place and all employees are aware of it, the best employees will seek out a mentor. They will also be the ones asking questions from everyone in order to learn more about the company and how it works.

The best employees will have more than one mentor, as they will understand that in order to advance they need to know about more than one section of the business. I have always had several mentors, and that has enabled me to work in many industry sectors. I have good knowledge of business finances and reporting, building management, health and safety, sales and marketing, customer relations, computer systems and a host of other disciplines.

Does the old saying about being "a jack of all trades, but master of none" apply? No it does not; I still consider myself an expert in training, communications and professional speaking. The other disciplines are additions that have helped my career progress.

I have had to learn some of those disciplines to a level where I could potentially work in that field. In most cases, I have enough knowledge to make sure that I can ask the right questions and understand the answers.

Wherever you are in the organisation, you need to know where you want to go and how to get there. Write out your destination, and then write out your roadmap for getting to where you want to go. Identify who you need to coach and mentor to fill the gap that you are going to leave. Identify the mentors that you will need access to in order to move up to the next rung.

Make sure that you stay on message. Are your goals aligned to the company and its vision? Are you able to transmit that vision down to those who will follow you?

Know your enemy

The management of all good businesses are constantly looking at their opposition to see what they are doing and what direction they are going in. Becoming the market leader in your business will never happen if all you do is follow what others are doing; you need to innovate as well. If you only innovate, you could have the best product on the planet, but if you don't do what the market demands, you could be left behind.

The business world is littered with products, which could have succeeded but did not. One of the most famous was Sony's Betamax video recorder. Launched in 1975, it had a monopoly in an emerging market. Five years later, it was down to a 25% market share, and five years after that it was no longer even a significant player.

JVC settled on the VHS system and launched their player with 2-hour tapes, rather than the 1-hour tapes that the Betamax used. VHS also had a slight price advantage, but industry experts say that this was not a significant factor.

JVC had looked at what their rival was doing and examined the market. They realised that the ability to record a complete movie on one tape was what the market wanted.

There were some small technical innovations in the VHS system, but the important factor was knowing what their opponents were doing and adapting to the market.

This is a clear case of looking at your rivals and taking action to beat them, but often it is not quite so clear-cut. Your enemies are not always your rivals, they are not always outside your company, you do not always know they are your enemy and sometimes they do not know they are your enemy.

The biggest enemy to a successful company comes from within. The vast majority of business are founded on a dream. Ford, Rockefeller, Carnegie, Branson, Gates et al, founded their business on a dream. Their dreams became so entangled with their companies that their visions continue to this day.

The problem comes when companies grow larger; the management becomes more complex and remote. Unless the visionary who founded the company is still in place and making sure that the vision is maintained, then the direction of the company can change dramatically.

Senior management are not necessarily working against the visionary; they will try to do their best for the company, in their own way.

Swissair was one of the world's iconic airlines and reckoned to be so financially secure and stable that it was known as the flying bank. Senior management decided to massively expand it through acquisitions funded by borrowing. They were so focused on this strategy that they had not allowed for a major change in the market. It was of course impossible to foresee the tragic happening of the terrorist attacks against the World Trade Centre on September 11 2001.

Other airlines survived this traumatic period, but being overburdened by debt through mismanagement meant the company folded six months later, after the Swiss government withdrew its support and set up a new airline.

Enron, Polaroid and Commodore Computers are all big companies started by visionaries, and all failed because management lost sight of the vision, did not pay attention to the market, did not talk to their customers or simply continued to do what they thought was right, sometimes in the face of overwhelming evidence that what they were doing was wrong.

This can happen on a much smaller scale within a company if the vision of the wizard that started the company gets lost in the hands of the warriors that are carrying out the day-to-day running of the company.

These warriors can be accidental enemies, but they are enemies just the same. Keep the vision alive, keep the wizardry going and potential enemies will remain as friends.

Chapter 7 Summary

A new business should be a magical process driven by a vision.

The founder of a new business will put heart and soul into it. It will be an all-consuming passion that sometimes subsumes everything else in the visionary's life. It is therefore important that everything and everyone around the business somehow serve the purpose of the business and its founder.

Employees, at least initially, have to be chosen with the greatest of care, so that everyone is driving in the same direction. One dissenting voice, while unlikely to kill a vision, can certainly delay its attainment.

Starting a business with one general and many foot soldiers is the best way for most businesses to start moving along. Eventually, a hierarchy is required, and the greatest of care is needed to make sure the right lieutenants are in place to make sure the army does not falter or make an inappropriate change of direction.

The key to a business's success is in its succession planning. A culture of quality, training, coaching and mentoring will almost certainly result in quality employees moving up the corporate ladder. As these employees climb the ladder, they are likely to maintain the company culture, which helped with their promotion and bring forth a new generation of quality employees who are happy to maintain the company vision.

Talk to your staff when changes in employees are being made. You cannot please everyone all the time, but through communication, you will please more people more often.

While a great vision is the way to get a company moving and growing, it is important not to lose sight of reality. The market still has to be watched, competitors have to be scrutinised and level-headed decisions need to be made.

The corporate world is awash with both businesses and people who have suffered spectacular failures from losing sight of the vision that was driving them forward.

If people cannot see or connect with the vision that is driving the company forward, then they can quite easily become unwitting enemies of the business. The enemy within is much harder to see and deal with than the enemy without.

Maintaining the magic and getting everyone working to keep that magic going will result in a successful business staffed by happy employees.

Chapter 8 Breaking The Chain

Lead from the top

As discussed in the previous chapter, most companies are built on one person's, or a small group's vision. In the early days, a business can thrive on the energy of the visionaries. That energy can carry a company through the crucial period of achieving enough growth and market penetration that it is likely to survive.

It is at this point that many businesses start to falter and stop growing.

This is generally because the business owner is scared to let go as there is no one that they trust enough to let them run their company. After all, it is a dream, and it is hard to put your dreams in the hands of someone else.

This is where great leaders need great communication skills. A leader needs to sit down with the team and explain why it is important that the primary goal of the business is to work towards the fulfilment of the company vision. Real leadership is about communicating the vision to the followers in such a way that they are not just happy to follow but are proud to follow and actively get on board with the company message.

The way to do this is to let people know in great detail what your vision is, why you want to achieve it and how you are going to go about it. When it is time to expand from that small core group, your role is going to have to change from team leader to manager, or perhaps even director, depending on how big you were at start-up and how big the expansion is going to be.

At that stage, you will become more remote from the people that you took on board at the start. They need to understand that you are going to introduce new roles and practices in order to ensure that your vision, the one they were so involved in, is realised. During the expansion phase you will need to create a new business plan, and this business plan will almost certainly be geared towards increased profitability. Loss making companies, or even those which break even, do not grow and will stop your vision in its tracks.

Do not hide this profitability from anyone in your company; instead, explain why it is so important to increase profits. Let people know that you are growing the company for your vision and that as a consequence, their jobs will be more secure and promotion prospects will be greatly enhanced.

Do not delegate these types of message. Write them yourself and deliver them to your workforce with the same passion that you used to talk about your vision when starting your business. Let your workforce know that your vision is not changing and that you are still in love with it.

Let your managers or team leaders know your content beforehand so that they can ask you questions about it and that they are prepared to interact with the workforce and in turn answer any questions that they might have.

Do not interfere – too much

The title of this chapter is "Breaking the Chain." I gave it that name because when a business grows, you have to implement a chain of command that can get quite lengthy. A typical business structure would be CEO, directors, managers, team leaders, supervisors and operatives.

As the CEO, you cannot be expected, nor is it wise, to be talking directly to operatives, supervisors and team leaders on a day-to-day basis. Your time is better spent on developing strategy and briefing your directors.

You need to make absolutely sure that your directors are on message and buying into your vision so that they can pass your leadership message down the chain.

Often though, directors are practical people who have worked their way up through the company structure. They may not have started on the shop floor, but they potentially started in junior or middle management roles and progressed from there.

There is therefore a high probability that they are not visionaries. If they were, they would probably be starting and running their own businesses, rather than working in yours. Being of a practical nature, there is every likelihood that they will translate your visionary message into more practical language before passing it on to the next level of the chain.

During this translation, there is every possibility that the message will become subtly changed and/or diluted. The vision of a CEO of a growing logistics company might be "to put a parcel in the hands of a customer within 24 hours of receiving the order." The message the director passes on to senior managers might be "We aim for 24-hour delivery."

Your managers are also likely to be practical people on a career track. They may be trying to get promoted or get a good annual review by making sure they avoid mistakes. The message they pass on may well be, "We need to be as quick and efficient as possible."

The team leader is often someone who is stuck between a rock and a hard place. They are trying to please the manager without alienating their team, who were probably co-workers until fairly recently.

The team leader is liable to tell the manager that they are an efficient team, doing their best. They will also likely compliment their team on a job well done, but may not even pass on a message as they are not seeing one.

This dilution of a message is a common business issue and one that can stunt growth and damage a company's reputation. To avoid this, the CEO must be asking for the correct executive summaries on a weekly, not monthly, basis. Thirty days is far too long to leave important issues to lie. The CEO needs to look for the Key Vision Indicators. These may well align with those tried and tested Key Performance Indicators, but they may not.

In our logistics company, a key performance indicator set by the operations director may be the number of parcels delivered within 24 hours of receipt. The Key Vision Indicator is likely to be how many parcels were in the hands of the customer 24 hours after the order was received.

This is when CEOs can break the chain and interfere a little. It is OK for the CEO to check directly with senior managers and find out what message they are working towards and how they measure their success. It is OK for the CEO to clarify what executive summary the board should be getting.

It is a difficult skill to do this without upsetting your directors or making them look bad in the eyes of their managers, but the good CEO will always find a way. Couch your request for a different summary as a favour. Apologise for making waves. Go to your operations manager and say something like.

"Sorry to bug you, but your director is busy. Could you do me a favour and set up a weekly report on the percentage of parcels that get delivered within 24 hours of the order being placed?"

No manager will refuse this, and they will not see it as a slight on a busy boss. They will be quite pleased that you trust them enough to come directly for "a favour."

Will this upset your director? Possibly, but they are a director and should have been giving you what you want. You should also have set ground rules that let your directors know that you will occasionally go to managers in order to avoid dilution of requests.

As long as you do not do this too often, there will not be a big problem at any level. If you have to do it too often, then you may have a poor quality director, are obsessed with micromanagement and cannot trust others with your vision, or you are not communicating your message properly.

If you keep your eye on your vision and constantly re-evaluate your message and your methods everything will work out.

Do the unexpected

Remember that being a visionary sets you apart from the crowd. You have a different thought process from those around you. As a business expands and you become a CEO, most people will expect you to conform to that position.

You will need to read sales reports, operations reports, profit projections and a host of other things that are needed to keep a company going in the right direction. You also need to let people see that you will not be completely conformist.

You are different from those around you, so make sure those people know it. Simple things like having meetings that don't need to be confidential in a café rather than in a stuffy board room will help maintain your image as a different thinker.

If you are a CEO that came up through the ranks, look in on your old team from time to time and buy them a beer after work or sit with them at lunch. When the CEO appears in the lunchroom, everyone will appreciate it.

For the smaller business, on a hot day go and buy everyone an ice cream. Do not send someone else out for it. Go get it yourself. That will build your reputation.

These little things mean a lot to people, and it keeps building your reputation as a caring CEO who does things a bit differently.

Bring one slightly off the wall or zany idea to every board meeting so that the directors know you are still innovating, and it might even encourage them to think differently.

Have team building days that are fun and make sure you take part. I once wrestled my CEO while we were both dressed in giant Sumo wrestling suits. It was the first bout in a team-building day. We were both useless and never got a result. The work force laughed about it for weeks, and even though they all had a go, the picture of the CEO and the operations director falling about in giant Sumo suits set the mood for the day.

As a teenager in London, I worked as a labourer on building sites. I was digging a drainage trench in sweltering hot weather when a well-dressed city gent appeared with two pints of ice-cold beer. He called me out of the trench and we stood chatting for about thirty minutes and enjoying the cold beers. He made pleasant conversation and asked about what I was doing, where I was from, what my future plans were and so on.

It turned out that he was the CEO of the Scott paper company, who at the time were the world's largest producer of tissues. It was part of a conversion on his London home that I was working on.

The last thing I could have thought about going to work that morning is conversing with a man of his stature on an equal footing. By doing the unexpected, he did not just make my day; he left me with a memory that has lasted for the rest of my life.

I have told that story many times, and while I don't suppose it will turn him into a bigger legend than his business status already had, it has left a lot of people with a positive opinion of him.

Doing the unexpected has a positive outcome for all concerned. It enhances your reputation and standing within your organisation and lets people know that you are still the visionary with the ideas that will keep the company going and their jobs secure.

Do the expected – a lot

Despite my encouraging you to communicate in unexpected ways by having fun and buying ice cream for the workers, it is still important for a CEO to do what is expected as much as possible.

People need to see that as well as being a fun and innovative leader, you do have the stuff that leaders need to have in order to run a successful business.

You need to be able to understand every part of your organisation and to talk knowledgeably with your directors and senior managers about it. Spend a lot of time analysing the business processes and get to know the flow of each department.

Ask directors and senior managers to explain their processes, find out everything from how leads for new business are generated to how your product leaves you and gets to the customer.

How are your invoices generated? How quickly do they get paid? How quickly do you pay your invoices?

This may all be stuff that you had a handle on in the early days when you were a small team and you had to do everything, but when a business grows, it is easy to lose sight of things. Everyone expects the CEO to know everything, to live up to his or her expectations and communicate with every department.

If your executive report from a department is late, chase it. Do not let people fob you off with excuses. When you are being the fun person with the ice cream, expounding your vision for the future, people may mistake this for vulnerability. Make sure everyone understands how important the business machine is and lead by example.

If you set up appointments and meetings with your management team, make sure you keep them. I have met CEO's who chop and change meeting schedules on a whim. Most often they will book appointments with new prospective clients or investors without referring to their diaries because they see new business or funding as more important than anything else.

The bottom line is that if you are giving out signals that show your staff as less important than anything else then you will not have a business to serve that new client or spend that funding on.

The fun and unexpected staff I wrote about in the last section is a great way to break up the monotony of everyday business tasks, and it is important to keep your business as people centric as possible. It is equally important that the routine business tasks are there to be broken up.

It is vitally important that the CEO is a figurehead of the company and that people outside the company look up to them as a visionary or thought leader. You need to make time to play that role and do the conferences, talks, and seminars so that you build a profile for your company.

The business market expects this, and you cannot run a business in isolation. Relationships built outside the company can lead to future joint ventures and alliances. Remember that you are aiming for the completion of your vision, and it may well be that when you achieve it the relationships you built along the way will help you towards your next vision.

As company leader and visionary, you will have to be different things to different people. Make sure that whatever you do, you are not only playing a part. You need to absorb yourself in business and let everyone see that you can do whatever is needed in any given situation.

Be approachable

Many years ago in the business world, almost everyone had an office. Internal real estate was a symbol of power and status. I once did some consultancy work for a company where every office was designed to be of a different size so that everyone knew where you were in the pecking order by the size of the office.

Promotion was automatic and based on qualifications and length of service rather than skill or competency. The result was a dysfunctional company with a much larger chain of command than was necessary.

I was viewed with great suspicion by the staff in the open plan area of the office, where I had a temporary desk. I could get up from my desk and walk into the finance director's office and ask him questions directly.

None of the accountants that I sat with had ever been able to do this, and they found it quite strange; one or two of the newly qualified accountants had never even spoken to him.

There was no sense of approachability in this company at all. Somehow it survived, but there was no joy in the office, and I am sure productivity suffered as a result.

Of course it is not appropriate for the CEO or even the directors to have an open door policy to every single worker in a large company, but the leaders must at least be seen as approachable by those a grade or two below them.

Business growth can only happen when the majority of people within the business are happy, productive and communicating effectively. This happens organically in small businesses because the management structure is so small and transparent. Most small businesses thrive because of the open door policy and the accessibility of the CEO to everyone.

The open door policy needs to exist in larger companies as well, but it needs to be a bit different. Everyone that works in a business should feel free to talk to his or her boss's boss. To not allow this sets a culture of elitism and can stifle ideas and employee growth.

The open door policy needs to be understood and implemented properly. An employee talking directly to a manager could upset the team leader who has been by passed. The manager needs to employ great listening skills and make sure that out of any discussion they have with an employee, there is a follow up discussion between the employee and the team leader, which may or may not involve the manager.

Everything depends on context and relies on all involved listening actively to understand the issues being discussed and the responses to those issues.

It has to be understood, in a non-derogatory fashion, that a team leader may be a team leader because they are not yet skilled enough to be a manager and that sometimes an employee needs to talk to someone higher up the chain.

The same applies at the top of a company. A senior manager may have a brilliant idea, which is quite visionary in nature, but cannot discuss it with a practical director. The manager needs to know that you as the

CEO are accessible for this type of discussion and the director needs to know that it is not a failure on their part when someone passes them by to talk to you.

The important thing is that when the conversation is over, the director gets involved in a follow up conversation so that they know what had been discussed. You never know; their practical input may have a bearing.

Chapter 8 summary

Are you leading from the top? Does every single person in your company know that you are not just running a business but that you are also driving a vision?

Is that message so powerful that everyone is on board with you and helping you to achieve your goals and dreams? Do they understand that achieving your dream is their future security?

When it is time to communicate with your staff about the business, do you write your own presentations? Do you write with your heart as well as your head?

Have you managed to trust your directors and managers enough that they are comfortable knowing that they can run their departments without risk of interference?

Do they also understand that ultimately it is your business and that on occasion you will need to ask questions and change procedures to make sure everything is aligned with your vision?

Do you still do the unexpected? Do you encourage company treats? Is there a budget for each department to give an occasional surprise to the staff? Do you occasionally make sure that everyone you work with knows that you are still that same visionary that started the business?

Despite being a visionary, have you mastered the practical aspects of running a business? Does everyone you meet know that you understand his or her department and how it runs? Are you seen as a steady hand on the tiller, steering the business consistently in the right direction? Are you carrying out all the day-to-day tasks of a CEO efficiently and professionally even though you take an occasional break to wrestle in a Sumo suit?

Have you continued with some version of the open door policy that took your business from start up to corporate? When people take advantage of the open door policy and bypass their line manager, is there a system in place that subsequently involves that line manager in a follow up conversation?

In short, are you ensuring that there is open communication throughout the organisation and that everyone in the business realises that this is because you are leading from the top?

Chapter 9 Empowering Your People

Empowering your managers

Empowerment is an often-misunderstood concept, and consequently it can scare people quite badly.

Many think that empowerment gives people free reign to run your business how they see fit, rather than how you want the business to be run.

Empowerment comes from making sure that people's job descriptions are accurate, both as written down and in the actual working practice, which can be different.

Job descriptions are designed to make sure that an employee at any level from shop floor to boardroom knows the absolute minimum that is expected of them, and details a range of tasks that must be completed. It should not be an exhaustive list of all possible duties and behaviours.

You would write in a job description for the operations manager that they will produce a report of the total number of completed orders that leave the premises every month.

You would not write in their job description that if an employee was feeling a bit down then they should make them a coffee and have a chat with them. You would still expect both items to happen.

Empowering managers is all about communicating that, as long as their department is producing what is expected and that they are on a route that aligns with achieving the company vision, they can pretty much run the department as they like.

The managers must of course also adhere to employment laws and company policies and stay within budget constraints. In return, the CEO needs to make sure that company policies are clear, managers know and understand employment law and that a suitable budget is in place with some leeway for ad hoc spending.

Empowerment only works if everyone in the management chain is working towards the company vision. It tends to fail if people are busy looking out for themselves.

Many years ago, I worked as a manager in a small training company. Both the CEO and my line manager were micro managers, and there were times when I felt that I did not need to be there, as they were effectively making all the major decisions. When the CEO retired, my line manager became director, and I became a senior manager.

We agreed that we would start an empowerment culture and enable managers to have a bit more control of their departments. Among the measures we implemented was a £50.00 threshold on purchases before higher authority was required.

The idea behind this was that managers could purchase training manuals and other materials without needing my sign off. This mostly worked well, as nearly everyone understood the reasoning.

One manager, who was not on message and did not stay much longer, simply ran amok and purchased all sorts of items, including a soft drinks fridge for his office, which no one else was allowed to use. He had a personal coffee pot, novelty phone and a few other gimmicks, which detracted from his work rather than enhanced it.

I did try to explain how empowerment worked, but he did not get it and eventually moved on to pastures new.

The amazing thing was that I did not even have to use a disciplinary process. The other managers ostracised him themselves, and it became uncomfortable for him to stay.

This is the real joy of empowering managers who are working with the company vision. They will support each other, and if someone does not play ball, they will become unpopular and are liable to move to an environment where they are more comfortable.

A company with an empowerment structure is a powerful organisation, but the CEO and directors need to ensure that results are being produced.

If your managers are fully empowered and good at what they do, then the company should grow organically and become more profitable due to those managers running their departments well and introducing improved efficiencies and working practices.

Sales managers will talk to operations managers and make sure that between them their departments are running at optimal levels.

If operations see that they have some slack time, they can ask sales to have a push to fill up the slack. If sales are running promotions, they will make sure operations are kept up to date with progress so that they can plan accordingly.

Empowerment, done correctly, leads to profit increases through efficiency and not having to waste time passing less important matters up and down a chain of command.

Empowering the work force

Empowering an entire workforce can be difficult and should be approached with caution in the larger organisations. Human nature and the law of averages suggests that there will be people who are never going to be on message, and giving them too much individual power without clear oversight could be a disaster.

Empowerment works best with small teams who communicate well and have a common purpose. As operations manager for a large IT training company, I only had five staff. None of us had set working hours. I never checked to see how many hours anybody worked, and no one ever put in a claim for overtime.

I had a departmental mission statement that simply said, "We do everything on time every time." Our biggest role was to make sure that every morning up 160 computers and desks were ready for use by delegates and that the in house restaurant was ready to provide them with coffee and snacks.

There was a natural rhythm required to achieve this, and everyone knew his or her part. It was not uncommon to be working at midnight on a Friday to make sure everything was set for Monday. My IT staff seldom worked more than an hour on a Tuesday and were almost never in the building before lunch time on a Thursday, and my catering staff seldom worked past 3:00pm.

Staff were perfectly happy to nip to the local computer store and buy replacement parts rather than wait for a delivery in the full knowledge that they would be paid back from petty cash the next day.

The end of an especially long and challenging day was usually completed with a free meal and a beer, because my director had empowered me to make those types of decisions.

Other departments had similar cultures, but they had more constraints. Training staff clearly had to be in the training centre during the day to train delegates and prep for their courses, but if they were not scheduled to train and had good facilities at home, they could learn new products without coming into the office. No one checked to see if they were actively learning or not.

As long as they had learned the next product by the time they were due to deliver, it wasn't an issue. I do not recall a single instance when a trainer turned up under prepared.

All this was only possible because our CEO told us that he wanted to have the biggest and best applications training company in the country. He involved us in any new strategy, explained his vision and made sure we got the message. We, in turn, explained this to our teams and worked with them until they understood that empowerment was a two-way street.

Having worked in a few empowered environments, I believe that empowerment favours the employer in terms of actual hours worked. In one empowered work place, I reckon I worked about a 60-hour week in the office and another 20 hours at home, while only being paid for 37.5 hours.

However, in return, that company gave me free use of resources, never quibbled when I used the printers or photocopiers for personal items and allowed me to stay after hours or come in at the weekend and use the internet back when it was still dial up modems and quite expensive to connect (we didn't have free local calls in the UK).

The net result of empowering a work force is that you generally get more productivity and a highly trained and motivated staff group.

As I said at the start, it is more difficult in some organisations. It is hard to empower someone who works on a production line and absolutely has to be there. However, it may be possible to allow a production line worker to learn a different role on the line and let them job swap. Do this enough, and you end up with a happier, multi skilled workforce.

During this process, you are also likely to discover who your next production line supervisor is. No matter what size your organisation is, it is worth at least looking to see where you can instigate or improve empowerment.

Done correctly and properly observed and supervised, an empowered work force will always lead to improved profitability and a better, more vision-focused structure within the business.

Carrots and sticks

The previous two sections about empowering the managers and work force within a company are mostly about "carrots," the reward system for encouraging acceptable behaviour and outstanding practice.

For the majority of basic grade employees and almost all managers, offering rewards is the best way to motivate and get a job done.

Rewards should be twofold: the expected reward and the (nearly) unexpected rewards. In a fully empowered organisation, the reward should be for getting the job done and not for turning up.

As a teenager, I worked as a labourer on building sites. My pay structure was threefold. I got a basic wage for turning up and being on site. I got an additional 15% for the time that I was actually working.

This meant that if it rained and all the work was outside digging trenches, I might have to sit in the shack and wait until the rain stopped.

I would still earn enough to eat, but reduced work meant reduced wages.

The third part was anything from an additional 15% - 30% for exceeding weekly targets. If it was my goal that week to dig 300 feet of trench and I dug 350 feet, I might get an extra 15%. If I dug 450 feet, I would get an extra 30%.

This was a good example of using the carrot. When it rained (and in the UK, it often does), I would regularly don some waterproofs and carry on working where possible. Most of my colleagues saw it as a stick they were being beaten with and felt they were losing money through no fault of their own. They ridiculed me for working in the rain for a measly 15% extra and encouraged me not to work, as it was exploitation.

Come the end of the week, they got a basic pay with a little bonus for what they worked on the non-rainy days. I got my basic pay, plus a full bonus for working and a productivity bonus, as I surpassed my targets by working when others would not.

I often got an additional bonus for helping out in foul weather. I remember working on the New London Bridge in 1973. Some steel girders had to be placed urgently as an expensive crane had been hired for the job. The rain came pouring down, and everyone retreated to the shack. No one answered a call to go out and direct the crane driver, who was nice and warm in his cab. I volunteered, albeit reluctantly as it would not add to my productivity bonus. I had waterproofs, and I did not want to spend the afternoon in a damp smelly shack drinking coffee and playing cards.

When the job completed that evening, the site manager thanked me and handed me a plain brown envelope, which contained slightly more than a full week's wages. Once I understood about the (nearly) unexpected bonus, I never hesitated to volunteer again.

This triple wage structure works well. Employees have the knowledge that come what may, they will have money on pay day, they know that if their job is done correctly they will have more money and they know that when they go the extra distance there is a chance that they will qualify for that (nearly) unexpected bonus.

I keep saying "(nearly) unexpected" because employees have to know that there is always a chance of that extra bonus, but they should never know for sure when or why they will get it. They need to know that superior performance will likely bring a reward.

Wage and bonus schemes like this should never be set up in a way that seems to penalise an employee for not achieving it. There needs to be clarity behind such a scheme. It also needs to be purely reward based.

One company that I worked for had a bonus scheme where everyone got a share of company profits over a certain level. To qualify to become part of the bonus scheme, staff had to achieve certain levels of competency. The more competencies a staff member achieved, the larger the share of the bonus they got.

When the scheme was first implemented, no one got any bonuses for the first two months, and there were many complaints. Meetings were held to help staff better understand the scheme and show them what could be done to help the company attain better profits.

The support staff started to engage with their customers to think about additional products, thereby increasing sales. Administrative staff cut down on wastage and sought better deals from suppliers.

Gradually, profits crept up, and bonuses started to be paid. As staff saw the scheme working, they engaged more and more and the bonuses increased.

New employees could only receive bonuses in their second year so that they understood it was reward based and not a built in part of the salary; otherwise it could seem that they were penalised on the occasional month when targets were missed.

The company ended up with a willing workforce all trying to improve company profits and working to improve their competencies. The provision of this carrot meant the stick never appeared. Any member of staff not working towards the goal was cajoled into action by the rest of the staff. If they did not respond to that cajoling, they tended to become isolated and more often than not left of their own accord.

Sometimes with employees, no amount of reward will motivate them or get them working on the message. This is when it is necessary to wield the stick of disciplinary procedures.

Excellence in communication is the watchword here, as getting a disciplinary action wrong can be costly, both in financial terms and workplace morale. It is absolutely essential that the employee handbook contains the disciplinary procedures and examples of what constitutes misconduct and what constitutes gross misconduct. You also have to be wary of precedents.

In many workplaces, it is considered gross misconduct to be at work under the influence of alcohol. It is also not uncommon in some workplaces for senior managers to have a glass or two of wine during a business lunch. If an employee was dismissed for being under the influence at work and could prove that the manager who fired them regularly had a liquid lunch, they would very likely win an unfair dismissal case.

Most disciplinary procedures go along the line of "verbal warning," "first written warning," "second written warning," "final written warning" and then dismissal.

These warnings are live on file for a set period. It is vital that you communicate to the employee, not the length of time, but the actual date on which a warning will expire.

It is also important that an action plan is put in place following each and every step in this procedure and that all parties sign off on that plan both at inception and conclusion.

Failure to communicate during the disciplinary process is a sure route to disaster. I have not had to deal with many disciplinary issues in my career, but when I have had to, my first step is always to add an extra step before the verbal warning, have an informal chat with someone and explain the disciplinary procedure to them. I also draw their attention to the relevant section in the employee handbook and let them know that they are getting a break.

In over thirty years of management, I have only had to dismiss one employee. I put this down to having good reward systems in place and only using the stick when absolutely necessary and, even then, wielding it as gently as possible.

Customers and Suppliers are people too

Empowering your team from top to bottom will definitely increase your profitability and ensure a happy, functional work place where people know that rewards are the way forward but are also aware that non-performance could result in the stick being shown.

Your customers are the easiest of all to empower. They already hold a lot of power and can vote with their feet by walking off to another supplier. As long as you recognise this and have successfully communicated to your employees the importance of the customers, you should not have much difficulty in retaining them.

Employees who engage well with customers will empower those customers to call them and discuss their issues knowing that you will offer a solution. Remember that companies do not buy from companies and people do not buy from companies; people buy from people.

People also do not want to buy products; they want to buy solutions to problems. Get your staff into the way of discussing a customer's problems with them, and you are no longer selling; you are empowering your customer to buy.

Every business owner dreams of having a product that is driven by their vision and has people queuing up to buy it because it solves a problem; in some cases it is a problem people didn't know they had beforehand.

The UK has quite a few low cost "no frills" airlines that fly them to all sorts of exotic destinations at prices they could not have dreamed of in the past. People fly from my native Glasgow to Latvia, Estonia, Slovenia and other places for less than they are paid for working one hour. No one ever considered this before, but by engaging with their staff and getting them all on the same message to keep prices down and have quality web sites, these companies have customers queuing up to fill their planes.

Being a "no frills" airlines was great, but woe betide the supplier who got it even a little wrong; customers would shift to another carrier in droves. Because this was a bit of a race to the bottom in terms of price, the carriers did get it wrong, and reputations suffered.

Now these carriers sell the frills at a premium, and customers are happy again. The extra legroom seats usually sell out before standard seating, and they now have to restrict the number of priority boarding tickets they sell as everyone was buying them.

Get it right and empower your customers to buy extras, and you will never look back.

Great businesses do this sort of “soft upselling” all the time. They do not try and hard sell the customers. They do not hold back essentials and make the customer pay extra for them. They do not hide charges. Everything is up front and open, which makes it easier to do business for both sides.

What about your suppliers? Are you empowering them to come to you with extras? I used to be responsible for getting packages out to customers in a timely manner. All the delivery companies looked much the same to me, so I chose the cheapest one. It seemed to work out OK. We did not have vast amounts of parcels to send, and we did not send stuff out every day.

I was quite pleased with the prices, and we had few problems with late delivery and never had a lost parcel. It felt like a win. What I had not factored in was the amount of time my administrator was spending on the phone organising collections. She came to me one day and said that she had a better solution, but that it was a little more expensive.

A potential delivery supplier had called to say that if we signed a yearlong contract (after a probationary period), they would supply us with packaging, bags, a printer, label rolls and would call at the office every day at 4:45 pm to see if we had anything that needed collecting.

When I looked at the pricing structure and weighed against the time my administrator spent buying supplies, wrapping parcels and ordering collections, it made sense to do it this way so I signed the contract.

Our current supplier called to see what had happened when they realised (three months later) that our business had dried up. I told them the story and they told me they could do the same thing for a similar price. I asked them why they had not offered it, and they told me they thought I was only interested in the cost.

Initially I thought this was their fault for not making the offer, but I eventually realised that I had never told them to call me and talk about any ideas they had for improving our relationship.

I now make a point of telling my suppliers that while it is important to control costs, it is equally important to improve the way business is done, and if they have any suggestions that may help, they should at least initiate a discussion.

My stationery supplier calls me every month to see what he can offer. Being a sole trader, I do not use much stationery, but I recently changed my office printer because he showed me one that could enhance my business process.

When it comes to empowerment, there are degrees to which you can empower different parts of your business, but at every stage, there is room for improvement so leave no one out.

Be as flexible as possible

Empowerment is about flexibility.

Within large organisations, empowerment can be difficult because people are so far away from the visionary that leads the company; they don't get the message no matter how hard people work to cascade that message down.

Sometimes in the small organisation, the opposite can be true. When people are as close to the visionary as they are at the start up stage, they will very likely take on some of the traits of the visionary. They assume that they are working in the same way. In fact, damage can be done by people using resources in good faith but with a false goal in mind.

I once saw a near disaster when someone decided to "help" recover some cash from overdue invoices.

They printed out the list and phoned each company in turn. They did the job well and brought in some much-needed cash. Unfortunately, they annoyed a good customer who had a 60-day term rather than the standard 30 days. The CEO had to work hard to recover a situation that he should never have allowed someone to feel empowered to deal with.

It is essential that there is never a "one size fits all" culture. Empowerment has to be selective and flexible. Departments should be able to empower their own staff, and there should be an understanding that not every department should be empowered to the same degree.

In the earlier example about me allowing the operations staff to work whenever they liked as long as all deadlines and quality measures were met, I did encounter resistance from other departments. They only saw the early finishes and late arrivals. They did not see the midnight oil being burned or the very early morning starts.

In particular, the administration department, who had to work from nine until five, felt a bit aggrieved. I worked with their manager, and between us, we came up with a scheme where they could have a bit more flexibility and by changing working patterns; they each managed to find a way of getting a day off every month in exchange for working an extra thirty minutes some days.

The key to flexibility is assuming that there is always room for improvement and discussing the tasks and procedures with the people that do them. Sometimes flexibility will not be possible. If you have a defined task that requires a strict approach for legal or safety reasons, it is vital that the task is treated as inflexible and that employee empowerment is sought elsewhere.

Once you have an empowered staff group and are checking that it is bringing rewards, keep looking for additional degrees of empowerment.

I once worked for a training department that was so empowered, the parent company spun us off as an independently managed subsidiary. This enabled us to sell our training courses outside of the parent company and generate increased revenue for the group while maintaining the standard of training that we had been supplying to them when we were an in house team.

All the group CEO ever saw of us after that was the monthly management reports that let him see that we were still doing OK and that profits continued to increase.

It is this type of flexibility that great leaders exhibit. We were not a core part of the group whose vision was to build the most luxurious homes in their target market while keeping the price in line with their competitors. Seeing things from a different angle allowed the group to continue their training programme and make additional money while sticking to their vision.

Chapter 9 Summary

Is your business built around flexibility and empowerment? Are you constantly trying to find new ways to help your employees work smarter?

As a business leader, you will have all the traits that are required to work on your own initiative. Do you easily recognise these traits in others so that you can focus on growing your vision while they are focused on running the business?

There is an overused saying, "Don't work in your business; work on your business." When you are a start-up, you often have no choice but to work in your business as well as working on it. As a business grows, the good CEO makes sure his people are empowered so that they work in the business while the CEO works on it.

Properly empowered managers and staff will also work on the business to improve it while they are working in it.

In short, an empowered company is a successful company.

Remember that the carrot is a lot more powerful than the stick. Genuine rewards will always engender results. Make sure that rewards look like rewards and are given out for improved performance rather than taken away for reduced performance.

If you have to wield the stick, and sometimes you will, then make sure you wield it softly but with precision so that you do not run into wrongful dismissal cases.

Make sure that you empower everyone you meet. There is no better asset to a company than a customer who feels empowered to buy extra services from you.

In the same way, you should always empower your suppliers to at least pitch ideas that they think can enhance your business. There will always be some suppliers that pester you by trying to sell you the same old solution. If you have truly empowered suppliers, they will come up with ideas to enhance your business, and the others will drift off into the twilight.

The key is flexibility and communication. Let everyone know that empowerment is on the menu, but that it may be different in different situations and for different departments. There is never a one size fits all solution, and remembering that and being flexible and open to ideas will mean a much happier, productive and profitable workplace.

Chapter 10 What Don't You Know?

Innocence vs ignorance

Ignorance is defined in the dictionary as *"lack of knowledge, information, or education."* Innocence is defined in the dictionary as *"lack of knowledge or understanding."*

The two words seem similar, and most people would prefer to be thought of as innocent rather than ignorant. This is mostly due to our childhood exposure to these words.

Being described as ignorant brings thoughts of being uncouth and ill-mannered. The word itself has quite a harsh sound; on the other hand, innocence has a soft sibilance about its pronunciation and conjures up pictures of being someone who is sweet an unspoilt.

The business reality is that we will always have a lack of knowledge. No one can possibly know everything. Ignorance is about not knowing, but understanding that you can learn. Innocence is about not knowing, but living in a bubble where you think everything is OK.

In 2002 American Secretary of Defence, Donald Rumsfeld said, *"Reports that say that something hasn't happened are always interesting to me because as we know, there are known knowns; there are things we know we know.*

We also know there are known unknowns; that is to say we know there are some things we do not know. But there are also unknown unknowns – the ones we don't know we don't know. And if one looks throughout the history of our country and other free countries, it is the latter category that tend to be the difficult ones."

If you are simply ignorant of a known unknown and a good business leader, you will pursue the knowledge that you need to turn it into a known known. As you pursue this knowledge, it is likely that you will stumble across items that you had no prior knowledge of (unknown unknowns). As soon as that happens, you have turned it into a known unknown and can again pursue a solution if one is needed.

If you are innocent of your knowledge, it is unlikely that you will even be aware of unknown unknowns, and it is probable that you won't try to resolve the known unknowns because in your innocence, you won't see the impact they may have on your business.

People who are innocent tend to be quite single-minded, and the carcasses of their failed enterprises litter the business highway. If you watch Dragons Den (Shark Tank in the USA), you see droves of innocents with what they think are brilliant ideas. Some of them have ploughed in their life savings and even re-mortgaged the family home to bring their dream to reality.

One would-be entrepreneur was somewhat devastated that his invention of an alarm clock that woke you by cooking bacon was immediately shot down as it was clearly a dangerous fire hazard.

Another could not understand when his invention of a device that plugged into a phone line and eliminated junk faxes was turned down. He had been working on it for ten years and simply had not factored in that so few faxes are now being sent that junk faxes have stopped anyway.

These are two stories of innocents who simply believed that their product was so good that they could not see why not everyone would want one. As a consequence of this innocent self-belief, they didn't do any market research.

Your market for a new product is a definite known unknown. The innocent will go to market anyway; the merely ignorant will do their market research and turn it into a known known.

Lifelong learning

Learning is the purest form of communication because it begins in the sub conscious as a nagging ill-formed message that you are missing something. It gradually forms into a conscious message that you can define and do something with. Once the learning is complete, you have a clear message going back into your brain as a solution to a problem and then down into your sub conscious as true knowledge.

Being a success in business can take a lifetime, and a business will only succeed when as many of those unknowns make the journey to becoming knowns.

Since we are torturing the mind with Donald Rumsfeld's awkward quote, let me introduce a similar mind twister regarding the pursuit of knowledge.

The journey to true knowledge is a four-stage process:

Unconscious incompetence – you don't know what you don't know.
Conscious incompetence – you know what it is that you don't know.
Conscious competence – you know what you know, but you have to work actively to implement it.
Unconscious competence – you know what you know, and can act instinctively on it.

When you take on board the idea of lifelong learning, not just for you but also for all staff within your business, you are starting work at step 1, unconscious incompetence.

Most businesses merely train their staff to do what needs to be done in order to get their job done. In industries where certification is a requirement, one of the most common questions asked on a training course is "Will this be on the test?"
This type of training starts at step two, conscious incompetence, and often stops at step three, where people are always actively having to think about what they are doing and how to implement the knowledge.

People only ever achieve step four, unconscious competence, when they learn through desire rather than need. Once the desire to learn becomes part of a person's psyche, they will have that desire for the rest of their life.

All successful leaders are readers. It is through reading, and other active forms of learning, that the unknown unknowns are discovered and that journey from unconscious incompetence to unconscious competence begins.

If you are in a business that needs staff to be certified in some way, then clearly this must be a priority. As a priority, it will of course be part of the employee handbook and communicated to the employee as a "must do."

It is important to go beyond the "must do" and enter the realm of "nice to do." Many companies, especially those involved in research, have ad-hoc programmes called 20% time or something similar. The idea is that employees get to spend 20% of their time working on side projects that are related to the core business. One such side project eventually became google mail. This is a great way to let people learn new skills and help the business at the same time.

Most employees who are exposed to this culture will spend more than the allotted 20% time on their side projects, as they will work on it outside standard hours as well. Again, everybody benefits.

As an IT trainer at one company, we had a theoretical 20% time to learn new software packages and courses. I learned most new software and courses on my own at home.

During my 20% time, I learned how to write computer programs to extract extra management information from the company's archaic database systems. This eventually led to my role as operations director.

Lifelong learning needs to be part of the company culture to make it work to the best advantage of the organisation and its people. Not everyone will buy into it, but those who do will become huge assets to the company.

It does cost money to run such a programme, but not as much as you might think. If you allowed a 20% culture in your company, then the figures suggest that you need five people to do every four jobs, and the wage bill will go up.

In reality, people who are learning in a friendly, supportive environment are liable to be more productive and will be working on their learning outside working hours as well.

Even if you do not run a 20% programme, you should still be training the staff and yourself by using courses, books, videos, seminars and online resources.

The outlay will always be less than the benefits.

Remember the answer to the question, "What happens if I train my staff and they leave?" is "What happens if you don't train them, and they stay?"

Own or rent?

Like everything else, knowledge is a commodity, and as such, it can be bought or rented. There may be knowledge that is needed to keep your business going, but it may well be better not to have that knowledge directly inside your business.

For most enterprises, the core knowledge that is needed to run a business exists within the employees and is effectively owned by the company, often as intellectual property (which you have registered, haven't you?). New employees coming on board are trained in the company knowledge, and clearly they benefit from it, but the knowledge still ultimately belongs to the company.

There are three ways to acquire new knowledge within a business. You and/or your staff can learn it in the ways described in the previous section. You can hire a new member of staff that has the required knowledge, and they will eventually cascade it to others in the business. These two options are effectively buying that information, as it will become part of the company procedures.

The third option is to rent the knowledge by employing a contractor or outsourcing the work to another company. A good example of this is payroll. Calculating an employee's salary is straightforward. Knowing what to retain for taxes, healthcare, insurance and other deductions is not quite so simple.

You can buy software that will perform this function, but you still need someone with the knowledge to run the software. Many small businesses buy the software and rent a contractor to come in for a few hours each month, or week, to run the payroll. Other businesses send off the timesheets to another company and let them deal with the payroll in its entirety.

The same applies to marketing and branding. Branding especially is something that does not need to be done every day, and marketing tends to be campaign based.

Most small companies will not be able to afford employing a marketing specialist full time and will rent the resources as and when necessary. Larger companies will have marketing departments but will still rent in skills if they decide to do a rebrand or are looking to run a special campaign.

So much business is now done online that it is almost essential for every business to have a web presence—not only a website, but social media as well. Knowledge such as how to best leverage LinkedIn, twitter, Facebook, etc. is unlikely to be core knowledge for most businesses, but it may be vital to have someone in house trained to make the posts. It may even be the same with your website.

It is important to have the knowledge that you must update all your online channels regularly, and you may have to buy this in house so that the updates are done with the insider knowledge that comes from being embedded in the business. It may also be important that you outsource the final content through a web savvy copywriter to ensure that the message is correctly constructed for each platform it will appear on.

In an ideal world, every business would have every function in house and have total control over all the knowledge that is required to run the business. The reality is that in today's business world if you tried to bring in all the skill and knowledge needed for every aspect of your business, you would have more ancillary staff than core staff, and more than 50% of your assets would be used on non-core functions, making your business unviable.

The basic idea is to buy and keep core knowledge and assets, and to rent or outsource everything else until you get to a size where it becomes cheaper and more effective to move it in house.

Talk to the market

Finding out what you do not know is not always easy. Paraphrasing the end of Donald Rumsfeld's quote – It's the unknown unknowns that prove to be difficult.

When it comes to the direction your business is going in, the unknown unknowns are all out in the market.

There are many companies out there that are shadows of their former selves or are gone completely because they did not see how the market was going.

Agfa, Kodak and Polaroid were all slow to see the impact that digital cameras, and eventually mobile phone cameras, were going to have on their industry sector.

Their issue was that they spoke to "experts" who said that they should not worry; there was no way that the quality of digital pictures would ever reach that of film.

They had good reason for thinking this. The early pictures were grainy and looked dreadful printed out. It was hard to see that there would be enough of an improvement to change this.

These companies also could not envisage a time people would not want their photos printed out. Last year, I took around 1,000 pictures and only printed three.

Had any of these companies gone out to the marketplace, spoke to the people and asked the right questions, they may have shifted focus much sooner and retained their place in the market.

I was an early adopter of the digital camera and would have been able to tell Kodak that the pictures were about memories and the quality was not massively important. I would also have told them it would only take a marginal increase in quality to have me completely happy with a digital camera despite the fact that the quality was so far behind that of a good glossy picture.

The instant gratification of the digital camera, especially when it arrived on our phones, was a huge selling point that film could never match.

Talking to the market and asking the right questions will always help you make sure you are going in the right direction.

What about bringing the market to you?

In my early days as a software trainer, we held open nights for our clients and prospects. We would have a formal demonstration of what we were working on and what our plans were.

This was followed by an informal buffet and drinks session, and the trainers and sales staff would mingle with the guests and answer their questions. From these sessions, we generated massive amounts of bespoke training business designed to meet a specific client's needs.

We then spoke to other companies in the same sectors and were able to provide them with similar services.

The market always knows what it wants, but unless you get involved with it, you will not find out. Communicating and using the right questions to your market is the only way you will find out.

Talk to your competitors

Before I get started here, let me make it clear that I am in no way suggesting a cartel or advocating anti-competitive practices. There is a huge difference between talking to your competitors and colluding with them.

I am also not suggesting that you talk to competitors to help you decide on pricing, manufacturing costs, etc. The market will take its own route to sorting these things out. It is important to not just be ethical but also be seen to be ethical and maintain the highest of standards.

Collusion is quite a dangerous game to play anyway. In 2011, several UK supermarkets and milk producers were fined a total of fifty million pounds for colluding over pricing and market sharing.

They were caught when an independent producer reported the fraud, after they found it impossible to sell their milk to supermarkets even though they were about 5% cheaper.

There is also a danger that someone outside a cartel will find a way to market, as Richard Branson did with Virgin Records, and undercut the whole sector, leaving cartel members in a difficult situation.

Talking to your competitors is about understanding the marketplace and ensuring there is enough space for everyone, including new players. It is also useful to know when to get out of a particular sector and when to stay.

There are few businesses where all the players are identical, so even if the competition know what you are doing, they will not necessarily be competing with you anyway.

Even supermarkets come in upmarket, mid-market and low end. Each one has their individual features, peculiar to its own markets. If you are talking to each other, you might find the high-end supermarket saying that it has had a downturn in ground beef sales so they are reducing stock. This might prompt the low or midmarket supermarket to ramp up its stocks, perhaps at the expense of dropping the higher priced steaks, which would be taken up by the high end supermarket.

This is not collusion or price fixing; it is a quicker response to the market trends at each level.

When I worked in the IT training industry, we regularly talked to our competitors to see where each of us was busiest and helped each other by transferring delegates from their courses to ours and vice versa.

There was no collusion involved, but it did mean that we kept costs down by not having specialist staff sitting idle with no delegates, while a competitor had delegates but no staff to train them.

Healthy competition is the lifeblood of business, and it is always good to have someone pushing us in the market. If you had a market all to yourself, you would likely become complacent. Of course, you should never give away confidential or market sensitive information, and any member of staff that has dealings with a competitor should be acutely aware of the boundaries.

Having good relationships with your competitors can help you survive in tough times as well.

One of our clients, a specialist printing company, had a fire, which completely destroyed their factory and its contents. Fortunately, they had a good back up of all their data, and they were able to retrieve a record of all their outstanding orders. They got their biggest competitor to fill the orders for them.

After I talked to them about this, their CEO told me that they would have gone out of business if they hadn't gotten their competitor to fulfil the order and that the competitor was happy to do the work because they got paid when the machines would otherwise have sat idle.

The competitor also didn't want to see our client go under as they often used their slack time when they had a big order, and they could ultimately lose business by not being able to fulfil future orders.

These conversations with your competitors should be kept informal and relatively public. Doing otherwise could be seen as potential collusion.

Your competitors will always keep you on your toes, so treat them with respect, and they will do the same for you. Who knows? You might end up getting extra business from them.

Chapter 10 Summary

The major goal of every business is to make money. You may be driving a vision, you may want to be the biggest player in the market, or you may want to sit in your own niche.

Whatever you do, you cannot do it without making money.

The only way you can make money is through knowledge. Knowledge of the market, knowledge of your own business and above all, the knowledge that you do not know everything are what will get you where you are going.

It is OK not to know stuff, but it is never OK to stop learning. Being ignorant is not a crime; it is a temporary state that you will resolve and return to time after time.

Learning in order to get a single task done is sometimes necessary and should be part of your business practice. Constant lifelong learning will set you and your business apart from the crowd and lead to success after success. It must not be learning for the sake of it; though that can be fun, any learning done in the business must be for the benefit of the business.

Examine your knowledge requirements closely. Own the core knowledge and rent the ancillary knowledge until you get big enough that it becomes cheaper to own.

The people that know the marketplace best of all are your clients and your competitors, so make sure you are talking to them and building relationships. Find out what your clients want and what they do not want anymore. Find out what your competitors are doing and what they have stopped doing.

The final words

Businesses thrive on communication, yet we constantly get it wrong.

Written communication, verbal communication and body language all contribute. No matter whether you are the CEO, a manager or a shop floor employee, you have a part to play in the success of a business. The extent of your part will only be felt and recognised through communication up and down the chain of command and out to your customers and suppliers.

Communication skills do not arrive accidentally; they have to be worked on. Every time you communicate, assess the message and its effectiveness strive for improvements at all times.

Messages are not always obvious. You need to make sure to declare important information in as straightforward and simple a way as possible. Never leave a message in someone else's care without checking that they understand exactly what you meant and that they are going to pass that message along in the intended fashion.

Be surprised if everyone understands your message the first time out; it does not happen too often.

Do not get dejected when people do not understand what you say. You may have to find different and multiple ways to say it, so that eventually everyone, or at least everyone who matters, eventually gets it.

Business communications are what makes the business work, so remember that no matter what you do or how you do it. No matter what other people think. It is your business, it is your message and...

It IS what you say.

About The Author

James McGinty is a Professional Speaker and Author.

After leaving school at 16 with few qualifications, James worked in a variety of manual jobs in the UK shipyards and on building sites. After quickly deciding that outdoor manual work in the harsh winters was not for him, he trained hard and became a telecommunications engineer.

While working in some of the poorest parts of Africa, James realised that perhaps telephones were not what people needed, and he moved back to the UK to become a social worker.

It was during this period that James realized that he had a knack for communication with both individuals and with groups of people. After five years in social work, James embarked on yet another career as a trainer and consultant.

While working as a trainer, James joined a public speaking club to enhance his presentation skills. He then became a keen competitive speaker, winning several UK and international championships.

As a trainer and consultant, James worked with most of the FTSE 100 companies, as well as several of the fortune 500.

After coming up through the ranks to become operations director with one of the UK's largest training companies, James decided to strike out on his own as a Professional Keynote Speaker, specialising in Business Communications.

James also runs workshops, carries out consultation work and trains people and groups in presentation skills.

If you would like to see him speak at your organisation or engage him for consultations or workshops, check out his website.

www.mcginty.net

Printed in Great Britain
by Amazon